LOAVES & FISHES

Foods From Bible Times

ABOUT THE AUTHORS—

Malvina Kinard is a teacher of gourmet cooking, as well as a gourmet cook herself. She is the busy head of Cook's Corner, Westport, Connecticut, a specialty shop which is now franchised in various cities throughout the country. Mrs. Kinard has written *The Kitchen Scholar* with Marjorie P. Blanchard.

Janet Crisler has long been a student of the Bible as well as gourmet cook and specialist in foods and herbs of ancient times. Mrs. Crisler, a neighbor of her coauthor, lives in Greenwich, Connecticut. Together, they have lectured and given demonstrations of many menus and recipes in this book before organizations and groups throughout the country.

LOAVES

& FISHES

Foods From Bible Times

MALVINA KINARD
and JANET CRISLER

Keats Publishing, Inc. New Canaan, Connecticut

LOAVES AND FISHES: Foods from Bible Times

Originally published in 1975 by
Keats Publishing, Inc.

Oenoke Edition published October, 1988

ISBN: 0-87983-466-8
Library of Congress Catalog Card Number: 75-19544

Printed in the United States of America

Designed by Ben Feder

Keats Publishing, Inc.
27 Pine Street
New Canaan, Connecticut 06840

"Give me neither poverty nor riches; feed me with food convenient for me."

SOLOMON, PROVERBS 30:8

CONTENTS

LOAVES & FISHES

Foods From Bible Times

ACKNOWLEDGEMENTS

Loaves & Fishes could not have been possible without the friendship, interest and cooperation of a great many people and organizations, and we are happy to make these acknowledgements:

To Dr. John C. Trever, internationally known for his part in the discovery of the Dead Sea Scrolls, and his wife Betty, for their encouragement and guidance through the controversial world of Bible scholarship; to Abu Issa, Palestinian archaeologist; to Adel Mosleh, school teacher at Samaria Sebaste in Israel, and author of *The History of Samaria*; to the Albright Institute Library at the American School for Oriental Research in Jerusalem, its Director, Dr. William Dever, and its Secretary, Nima Jibrail, who introduced us to the world of cooking with *leben* and its complicated recipes.

Dr. Robert J. Bull, Director of the Archaeaological Expedition to Caesarea Maritima, Israel, and his wife, Dr. Vivian Bull, opened many doors to us, leading us into a new world of biblical research; Professor Benjamin Mazar, dean of Israel archaeologists, and Director of Excavations in the Old City of Jerusalem, showed great interest in our work, and gave us their permission to reproduce the striking bread seal on Page 113. His secretary and daughter-in-law, Mrs. Esther Mazar was helpful to us on numerous occasions. Our thanks must be expressed at this time to Dr. Avi Itan, director of the Department of Antiquities of the Israel Museum, and other Museum authorities for the many opportunities to view the finest antiquities relating to the background for this book.

Abu Musa and Mike Hawa, Palestinian guides and drivers, spent endless hours answering our questions, and introduced us to a Bedouin family who showed us how to make unleavened bread in their home at Dahab on the Red Sea. Mrs. Munira Said, teacher of Middle Eastern cooking in Jerusalem, contributed the ancient Taboon chicken recipe which we have used, in addition to spending so much time explaining techniques of ancient cookery, some of which are still practiced in the countryside today. David Issa and George Noursi showed us the many ways the flat bread recipe is prepared in the Old City of Jersualem.

Our appreciation, too, must be expressed to the Zion Research Library in Boston, Massachusetts; and to the Rockefeller Museum and Library in Jerusalem where Mrs. Pomerantz was so helpful.

Finally, for his continuing encouragement, we express thanks and deep gratitude to Cobbey Crisler, husband of one coauthor and dear friend of the other.

PREFACE

Loaves & Fishes will be a delight to many readers, both for its many glimpses into unusual details concerning the culinary customs of biblical times and for its many fascinating suggestions about unusual dishes that will challenge the imaginations of housewives and church-dinner gourmets. Intended as a biblically-oriented cookbook, it goes beyond the usual pages of recipes to mingle bits of historical glimpses into Bible times with touches from archaeological discoveries relating to festivals, foods and eating.

A product of the fertile imaginations of two enterprising women who combine their culinary skills with gourmet sensitivities, the book is a rare combination of history, literature, anecdotes and unusual recipes for Western tables.

This book is not intended for scholars, nor could it be called scholarly; but even the scholar might enjoy some of the tempting suggestions for kitchen experiments that would add zest to sober discussions around the dinner table.

Each brief chapter of the book is introduced by a biblical passage, commentary and a suggested related menu commensurate with the status of the person in the chosen story, such as Solomon, Herod the Great, John the Baptist, Archelaus and other Bible figures. What the authors have accomplished in *Loaves & Fishes* is a delectable compendium of tasty treats provoked by biblical literature.

John C. Trever, Ph.D.
Berea, Ohio
August, 1975

INTRODUCTION

The Bible has been the source of information and inspiration for countless numbers of people through the centuries. Our deep interest in the history of food led us, quite naturally, to the Bible. In it we found, to our delight, a definite correlation between ancient and modern foods. For instance, in the book of Ezekiel, we discovered a "recipe" for making bread, naming ingredients which may be readily purchased today.

In prehistoric times, the search for food was an impelling force in shaping the history of mankind. Later, religious codes greatly influenced the preparation of foods and the people's eating habits. The ancient countries of Syria, Assyria and Babylon developed a highly sophisticated culinary tradition. By New Testament times, entertaining in Greece, Rome and the Middle East had become extremely lavish and varied.

From the facts in the Bible about the food and domestic life of its people, and from works of history and archaeological findings, we have been able to adapt what we feel to be foods representative of the periods we have chosen as well as familiar to contemporary cooks. While some information on cooking methods of the past has been discussed, we have not tried to make each recipe totally accurate historically. Baking bread on stones or boiling meat by dropping red-hot rocks into the pot with it is possible, but likely to discourage the modern cook. Also, some present-day ingredients have been used to substitute for antecedents now unavailable. Capitalized recipes in the text may be located by consulting the Index.

We have aimed at presenting equivalents of dishes of biblical times, hoping by the ancient communion of food to bring to remembrance the meaning of the lives of the people who once were nourished by those dishes.

We hope you will enjoy our findings and as these recipes carry you back to the original pages in the Bible, you may find, as we have, far more inspiration and joy. The Bible is a marvelous storehouse of knowledge about those long-ago people. As they cultivated their land and prepared their meals, they were confronted by the same moral and spiritual challenges that face twentieth-century thinkers.

After all, the Bible has been rightly called "the greatest book in the world," and who knows—you may discover that the food in its pages is truly food for thought.

Malvina Kinard
Janet Crisler

Several recipes in this book call for herbs and spices which may be hard to find locally. A card to the publisher will bring you specific information as to where they may be obtained.

From the Old Testament

CHAPTER ONE

NOAH

"And the Lord said unto Noah, Come thou and all thy house into the ark; for thee have I seen righteous before me in this generation . . . And take thou unto thee of all food that is eaten . . . and it shall be for food for thee, and for them" (Genesis 7:1; 6:21).

Menus

I

Noah on the Ark

WATERCRESS SOUP

OMELET

CHICK-PEAS WITH TAHINI

UNCOOKED NUT CRESCENTS

II

Noah on Mount Ararat

ARARAT LAMB

TURNIP BASKETS WITH PINE NUTS

CABBAGE SALAD

PITA BREAD

ZIMRAH COMPOTE

III

Noah, the Food-Gatherer

BLACK SEA CASSEROLE

BARLEY PILAF

WILTED CUCUMBERS

DATE PALM PUDDING

IV

Noah, the Vine-Dresser

VEGETABLE SOUP

POST-DILUVIAN CRAB SALAD

GRAPE CONSERVE

SWEET CURD PIE

NOAH

"And it came to pass after seven days, that the waters of the flood were upon the land" (Genesis 7:10).

To provision the Ark for eight people for one year and eleven days—leaving out the immense amount of feed for two each of every kind of animal!—must have been a massive undertaking. Fresh meat was ruled out, of course, though there would have been reasonable quantities of eggs and milk, so Noah and his family would have had to rely on vegetables, grains and fruits for the long voyage.

If we were to place Noah in actual history, he would belong to the period between the Neolithic and Chalcolithic ages—very roughly, 4000 B.C. At that time, excavations and studies have shown, men were nomadic, following animals over migration routes and beginning to domesticate them. Grains and wheat were grown and provided coarse flat bread; about 6000 B.C. bread wheat had appeared, with its marvelous gluten content, allowing raised bread.

The people of Noah's time continued to bake flat bread as well—as many Near Eastern nations do today—on embers with hot stones placed on top of the loaf for even heat, a method still in use among Bedouin tribes along the Red Sea and in Sinai.

Before the Flood, Noah and his family in their nomadic life would harvest the wild fruits of trees and vines in their seasons, and gather snails, crabs, mussels and turtles to vary their fare. For their stay in the Ark, they would have stored herbs, grains, fruits, and nuts, and sought ways to vary their diet by pleasing combinations and the use of eggs and milk provided by their livestock. They probably made goat's cheese using a churn shaped like a bird. Ropes were drawn through two holes at either end and suspended from posts—

substitutes on the Ark for trees—and the churn was rocked like a cradle until the cheese was formed. Menu I reflects the available food, prepared with modern adaptations of the techniques revealed by archaeology to be in use at the time.

When the waters of the Flood receded and Noah came forth from the Ark, he sacrificed to the Lord, and, we must assume, followed the custom of setting forth a thanksgiving feast, using the portions of the sacrificial animal that were not burnt upon the altar. Menu II is a reconstruction of what this feast might have been.

With a world to replenish, Noah and his sons had much to do—to reestablish the art of agriculture, and to extend it, to sow and harvest. While they were waiting for their first fields and vines to bear, they had their stores to rely on, and the resources of the sea, now once again a provider of food rather than the death-shroud of the world that had gone before. Menu III suggests the kind of food that might have been eaten during this period; and Menu IV shows what the newly revived earth could provide at harvest time.

The lives of the nomads had become pastoral and prosperous. We may feel that the Lord's covenant with Noah was a promise of the enjoyment of the fruits of the earth for his family and for future generations: "I do set my bow in the cloud, and it shall be a token of a covenant between me and the earth" (Genesis 9:13).

I

Noah on the Ark

WATERCRESS SOUP

1 medium potato
6 cups rich chicken broth
1 bunch watercress
Salt and white pepper
2 cups light cream (optional)

Peel and dice potato. Cook in 5 cups chicken broth until tender (about 10 minutes). Discard stems of watercress. Place leaves in a blender with remaining 1 cup chicken broth. Cover and whirl until finely chopped and smooth. Combine with broth and potatoes. Season to taste. Add cream, if desired. Serve hot or cold.

Makes 6 to 8 servings.

OMELET

2 eggs
½ teaspoon water
½ teaspoon butter
Salt and pepper to taste
1 teaspoon chopped mint (optional)
1 teaspoon chopped parsley (optional)
Caviar Filling (recipe follows)

Break eggs into a bowl. Add water and beat until mixture is frothy. (If Caviar Filling is not used, add herbs to beaten eggs.) Place a heavy 10-inch omelet pan over high heat and allow it to get very hot. (Drop a bit of water into the pan. If it dances and evaporates at once, the pan is hot enough.) Place butter in the pan and swirl it around to cover the surface. Pour in eggs and at once start to stir them with the flat side of a fork in a swirling motion. At the same time, shake the pan with a fore-and-aft motion. When the mixture is no longer liquid, let the omelet rest a moment. Spoon Caviar Filling down center. Fold omelet and roll it out onto a warm serving plate.

Makes 1 serving.

Caviar Filling

1 tablespoon chopped parsley
1 tablespoon sour cream
1 tablespoon red caviar

Combine ingredients and mix well.

CHICK-PEAS WITH TAHINI
(Chick-Peas with Sesame Sauce)

1 can (16 ounces) chick-peas
3 tablespoons tahini (sesame seed paste)
Juice of 1 lemon
1 clove garlic
1 teaspoon salt
⅓ to ½ cup water

Rinse chick-peas in a colander and drain thoroughly. Place in a blender with other ingredients. Cover and blend thoroughly until mixture becomes a smooth paste. Use as a dip for raw vegetables.

Makes 6 to 8 servings.

Noah

UNCOOKED NUT CRESCENTS

1 cup zwieback crumbs
2 cups finely chopped walnuts
½ teaspoon cinnamon
1 teaspoon vanilla
2 egg whites
1¼ cups confectioners' sugar

Combine crumbs, walnuts, cinnamon and vanilla with unbeaten egg whites. Roll into small crescents or balls; dredge generously in confectioners' sugar. Allow to dry on wire racks for several hours.

Makes about 2 dozen cookies.

II

Noah on Mount Ararat

ARARAT LAMB

3 to 4 tablespoons oil
3 pounds boneless lamb, cut in 1-inch cubes
3 tablespoons flour
2 tablespoons sugar
3 cups stock or water
1 bay leaf
½ teaspoon rosemary
Salt to taste
1 cup diced turnips
12 pearl onions
4 carrots, cut in strips
1 cup lima beans

Heat oil in a heavy skillet and brown lamb on all sides. Sprinkle with flour and continue browning. Sprinkle with sugar and allow it to caramelize (this adds a fine color to the stew). Add stock or water, bay leaf, rosemary and salt to taste. Simmer about 45 minutes or until meat is tender. Let stand 15 minutes, then skim off fat. Add vegetables and cook 30 minutes longer. Correct seasonings and serve immediately.

Makes 6 to 8 servings.

TURNIP BASKETS WITH PINE NUTS

8 medium turnips
4 tablespoons butter
½ cup diced celery
½ cup toasted pine nuts
Salt and pepper to taste
1 cup buttered bread crumbs

Peel turnips, but leave them whole. Boil in salted water until just tender (about 30 minutes). Allow to cool slightly, then scoop out centers leaving a space for filling. Melt butter in a skillet. Add celery, and cook until tender. Add pine nuts, salt and pepper. Fill turnips with celery-nut mixture and place in a shallow baking dish. Sprinkle generously with bread crumbs. Bake at 325 degrees for 10 to 15 minutes, then brown under broiler.

Makes 6 to 8 servings.

CABBAGE SALAD

4 cups shredded cabbage
1 cup chopped apple
½ cup mayonnaise
½ cup sour cream
2 tablespoons lemon juice
2 tablespoons fresh mint
1 teaspoon celery seeds
1 teaspoon sugar
1 teaspoon salt (or to taste)

Combine cabbage and apples in a large bowl. Combine mayonnaise and sour cream; then stir in remaining ingredients. Add to cabbage mixture and toss lightly. Correct seasonings.

Makes 6 to 8 servings.

PITA BREAD

1 package active dry yeast
1 teaspoon sugar
1⅓ cups lukewarm water (about)
4 cups flour
1½ teaspoons olive oil
1 teaspoon salt
½ cup cornmeal

In a large bowl, combine yeast, sugar and ¼ cup of the lukewarm water. Mix thoroughly and let stand 5 minutes or until mixture starts to bubble. Add flour, olive oil, salt and remaining water. Stir mixture by hand or with an electric beater until well combined. Dough should be firm but not stiff. Add more water, if needed.

Knead dough until smooth and elastic. Shape into a ball and place in a greased bowl. Cover with a towel and allow to rise until double in bulk, about 45 minutes. Punch down and divide into 4 equal parts. Cover and let rise again for 30 minutes.

Preheat oven to 500 degrees. Sprinkle 2 large baking sheets with cornmeal. Roll each ball of dough into a circle about 8 inches in diameter and no more than 1/8 inch thick. Arrange on prepared baking sheets. Cover again and allow to rise for 30 minutes.

Bake loaves on lower shelf of preheated oven until puffed and brown, approximately 7 to 8 minutes. Remove from oven, wrap each loaf in foil and set aside. Bread will fall, leaving a shallow pocket of air in center. Serve warm or toasted.

Makes 4 flat loaves.

ZIMRAH COMPOTE

1 cup dried apricots
1 cup dried apples
1 cup seedless raisins
½ cup unblanched almonds, coarsely chopped
¼ cup pistachio or pine nuts
1 cup sugar
¼ teaspoon almond extract
1 cup heavy cream, whipped

Place whole fruit and nuts in a deep bowl and cover with hot water. Add sugar and almond extract. Let fruit soak until a golden rich syrup develops (about 48 hours). Serve in tall-stemmed glass goblets and top with a dollop of freshly whipped cream.

Makes 6 to 8 servings.

III
Noah, the Food-Gatherer

BLACK SEA CASSEROLE

3 shallots, finely chopped
1/3 cup lemon juice
6 tablespoons butter or margarine
6 tablespoons flour
2 teaspoons curry powder (or to taste)
3 cups milk
Salt and pepper
Hot mustard
1 pound shrimp, cooked and cleaned
1 cup lump crab meat
1/2 cup chopped lobster meat
Buttered bread crumbs

Simmer shallots in lemon juice until liquid is slightly reduced. Melt butter or margarine in a saucepan. Add flour mixed with curry powder and cook, stirring, until well blended. Gradually add milk and cook, stirring constantly, until sauce is smooth and thickened. Season to taste with salt, pepper, mustard and shallots. Gently stir seafoods into sauce. Correct seasonings. Spoon into shallow casserole and sprinkle top with buttered crumbs. Bake at 350 degrees 20 minutes or until heated through and crumbs are brown.

Makes 6 to 8 servings.

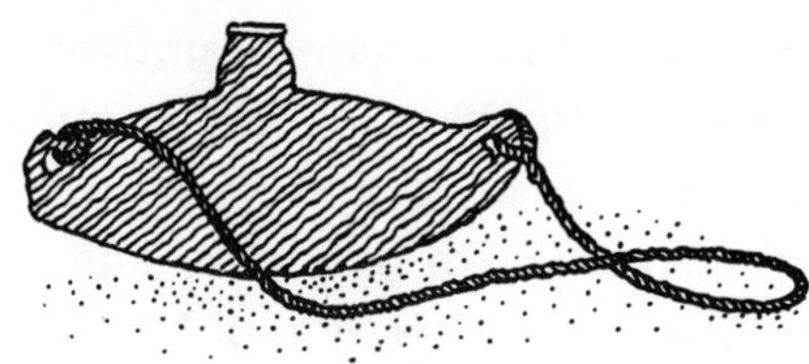

BARLEY PILAF

¼ pound butter
1 medium onion, finely chopped
1 cup barley
3 cups chicken broth
1 cup cottage cheese
1 cup sour cream
Salt, pepper to taste
Chopped parsley

Melt butter in a large skillet. Add onion and toss until soft. Do not brown. Add barley and stir well to coat with butter. Cook over medium heat until barley starts to turn color, then add 3 cups chicken broth. Allow to simmer until barley is tender (about 35 minutes). Transfer to a large casserole and add cottage cheese, sour cream and seasonings. Cover and bake at 350 degrees for 45 minutes or until all liquid has been absorbed and barley is firm but tender. Garnish with chopped parsley.

Makes 6 to 8 servings.

WILTED CUCUMBERS

4 to 5 cucumbers
2 to 3 tablespoons salt
½ cup Basic Salad Dressing
Freshly ground pepper

Choose firm cucumbers with untreated skins, if possible. Cut unpeeled cucumbers in half lengthwise. With a sharp spoon, scrape out seeds and discard. Slice cucumbers as thinly as possible. Place in a bowl and sprinkle generously with salt. Place a plate over top of bowl and shake vigorously several times. Turn cucumbers into a sieve or colander and rinse thoroughly in cold water. Drain well, then place in a glass serving dish. Add dressing and a sprinkling of freshly ground pepper. Chill.

Makes 6 to 8 servings.

DATE PALM PUDDING

4 cups cold milk
½ cup rice flour or cornstarch
6 tablespoons honey
1 teaspoon vanilla
1 teaspoon cinnamon
½ cup chopped pitted dates
½ cup chopped walnuts
Dash of salt

Mix a small amount of milk with flour or cornstarch to make a smooth paste, then add remaining milk. Cook over medium heat, stirring constantly until mixture thickens. Add honey, vanilla and cinnamon; blend thoroughly. If mixture is too thick, add additional milk to achieve desired consistency. Add dates, walnuts and salt. Chill in serving dish.

Makes 6 to 8 servings.

IV

Noah, the Vine-Dresser

VEGETABLE SOUP

1 soup bone with meat (about 2 pounds)
3 quarts water
Few celery tops
1 onion, sliced
3 sprigs parsley
1 bay leaf
½ cup raw barley
1 cup fresh sliced leeks
1 cup lima beans
1 cup chopped turnips
Salt and pepper to taste

Cover soup bone with water and add celery tops, onion, parsley and bay leaf. Simmer 2 or 3 hours or until meat is tender. Allow to cool; remove fat from surface, then strain. Discard vegetable bits. Remove meat from bone and add to stock. Bring to simmer again and add barley. After 15 minutes, add leeks, lima beans and chopped turnips. Simmer 45 minutes or until slightly thickened. Season to taste.

Makes 6 to 8 servings.

POST-DILUVIAN CRAB SALAD

3 cups crab meat, picked over well
Juice of 1 lemon
3 tablespoons chopped scallions
½ cup mayonnaise (approximately)
Lettuce
3 hard-cooked eggs, quartered

Combine crab meat, lemon juice and scallions. Add enough mayonnaise to bind, mixing lightly. Place on lettuce leaves and garnish with quartered eggs and additional mayonnaise.

Makes 6 to 8 servings.

GRAPE CONSERVE

4 pounds purple grapes
Grated rind and juice of 2 oranges
5 cups sugar
1 cup raisins
Pinch of salt
1 cup chopped walnuts

Wash grapes and remove stems. Slip off skins and reserve; place grape pulp in a saucepan. Cook pulp over low heat 6 to 7 minutes, then press through a coarse sieve to remove seeds. Discard seeds; return pulp to saucepan. Add orange rind and juice, sugar, raisins and salt, and continue to cook over low heat, stirring to avoid scorching. When mixture begins to thicken, add grape skins and continue cooking 6 to 8 minutes or until quite thick. Add walnuts. Pour into sterile hot jars and seal while hot.

Makes about 3½ pints.

SWEET CURD PIE
(Cottage Cheese Pie)

Crust

1¼ cups zwieback crumbs
¼ cup sugar
½ cup melted butter

Combine crumbs, sugar and melted butter. Toss with a fork until butter is absorbed. Press into a 9-inch pie plate. Chill before using.

Filling

2 cups creamed cottage cheese
2 tablespoons gelatin
½ cup cold water
Juice and grated rind of 1 lemon
Dash of grated nutmeg
½ teaspoon salt
2 eggs, separated
½ cup plus 2 tablespoons sugar

Press cottage cheese through a sieve to remove all lumps. Soften gelatin in cold water, then set over hot water to dissolve. Add to cottage cheese with lemon juice and rind. Season with nutmeg and salt. Beat egg yolks with 2 tablespoons sugar until pale and light. Add to cheese mixture. Beat egg whites, adding ½ cup sugar gradually, until glossy and stiff. Fold into cheese mixture carefully. Pour into prepared shell and chill several hours or until firm.

Makes a 9-inch pie.

CHAPTER TWO

MOSES

"And the house of Israel called the name thereof Manna: and it was like coriander seed, white; and the taste of it was like wafers made with honey" (Exodus 16: 31).

Menus

I

Moses in Pharaoh's Palace

CREAM OF ALMOND SOUP

RED SEA SCALLOPS IN SHELLS

GREEN BEANS VINAIGRETTE

FAYYUM RICE (CHUTNEY RICE)

PICKLED MELON OF THE NILE

LEMON CAKE PUDDING

II

Moses in the Land of Goshen

PATRIARCHAL POTTAGE
(LENTIL SOUP)
GOSHEN MEAT LOAF
CELERY ROOT PURÉE
COILED SNAIL ROLLS
CAROB DELIGHT

III

Moses in the Wilderness of Sinai

SINAI QUAIL WITH CHERRIES
CABBAGE IN SOUR CREAM
BARLEY WITH ALMONDS
BITTER HERB SALAD
WITH
WILDERNESS SALAD DRESSING
MANNA

IV

The Promised Land

BUTTERFLY LEG OF LAMB
BROAD BEAN CASSEROLE
FRUIT SALAD
WITH
PROMISED LAND SALAD DRESSING
BEATEN BISCUITS
CHEESE TORTE

MOSES

"And the child grew, and she brought him unto Pharaoh's daughter and he became her son. And she called his name Moses: and she said, Because I drew him out of the water" (Exodus 2:10).

Born a Hebrew but raised as an Egyptian prince, Moses enjoyed all the luxury and privilege that the ancient world had to offer. The Bible records little of this early period of his life, but the church father, Irenaeus records the tradition that he "was appointed general of the army against the Ethiopians, and conquered them and he married the king's daughter, because out of her affection for him she delivered the city up to him."

If this happened, Pharaoh would certainly have rewarded the victorious Moses with a triumphal banquet accompanied by royal entertainment, games, music and the finest food—and even if the story is unfounded, Moses would have attended such a banquet given for another as a member of the court, a lavish experience very far from the rigors of his later life in the Wilderness.

An Egyptian royal banquet followed a set, traditional, but highly festive course.

Guests would arrive at the palace about noon in chariots, on foot, or carried on palanquins. They would enter rooms scented with myrrh or frankincense; servants would anoint their heads with sweet-scented ointments, and if they had had a long journey, water in gold basins would be brought to bathe their hands and feet. Musicians played the harp, lyre, guitar, tambourine, pipes and flutes and, according to Herodotus, toasts were drunk from brass or bronze goblets.

Wine was presented to a woman following a special ritual: a servant brought it in a small vase and poured it into a drinking cup. He then gave the cup to a slave who presented it to the woman. Men received their libations directly in a one-handled goblet. When a guest had finished drinking a cup of wine, a servant gave him a napkin, refilled the cup or goblet and repeated a kind of benediction—"May it benefit you." This custom is still practiced today in the Middle East.

Pharaoh and his queen always sat together on splendidly carved chairs, formally greeting each guest. As dinner began, a variety of hors d'oeuvres were served, including a crude form of cabbage thought to stimulate a desire for wine. A soup such as cream of almond or lentil followed, particularly since soup spoons of ivory, alabaster or bronze were just being introduced at this time. Dinners were leisurely affairs and went on for hours for good reason, for the meat was slaughtered only as the guests arrived.

Goose, the favorite national dish, would inevitably be served, but there also would be a great selection of wild goat, kid, gazelle, teal, quail and other birds as well as fish. Sheep wool was so valuable that lamb or mutton were never used for food in Egypt. Celery root was one of the favorite vegetables among the many that grew along the fertile banks of the Nile valley.

In the royal dining-room long tables were piled high with fresh fruits, breads and pastries. Bread was shaped into coiled snails or recumbent cows or other animals—perhaps the first kind of animal crackers. The walls of the tomb of Rameses III at Thebes show paintings of the entire baking process from bare feet tramping out the dough in a kneading trough to the huge ovens made of Nile mud.

Each course was served on small round tables, one for each guest. Beer and wine constantly accompanied the food. A wall painting in one Egyptian tomb shows an open recipe book, listing ten varieties of meat, five kinds of birds, sixteen kinds of bread and cakes, six kinds of wine, four kinds of beer and eleven kinds of fruit.

At the end of the meal, Pharaoh expressed proper gratitude to the gods. A wooden statue of Osiris, god of the underworld, might be passed among the guests to remind them of the transitory nature of life. Then the entertainment began—music, singing girls, tumbling acts, games of chance, odd-and-even finger throwing—called Mora—and draughts. Pictures on the tombe of Rameses III show the Pharaoh playing dice with ladies of his court.

Menu I will allow the modern cook to re-create some of these splendors—though you will probably not want to anoint your guests' heads with oil or provide them with a series of vaudeville turns!

Moses lived in and presumably enjoyed this glittering world for the first forty years of his life; but then he became aware of the oppression on which it was founded. "And it came to pass when Moses was grown that he went out unto his brethren, and looked on their burdens; and he spied an Egyptian smiting an Hebrew, one of his brethren. And ... he slew the Egyptian and hid him in the sand. Now when Pharaoh heard this thing, he sought to slay Moses, but Moses fled from the face of Pharaoh, and dwelt in the land of Midian" (Exodus 2:11, 12, 15).

After Moses escaped into the desert, he was befriended by the priest of Midian, Jethro, whose daughter Zipporah he married. Moses tended his father-in-law's flocks, learning to live in an arid, uninhabited region with only his herds for company. We can assume that his diet was much like that of any pastoralist, and have suggested what it might be in Menu II. (The lentil soup, or "pottage" is, of course, also associated with Jacob and Esau—it is nourishing, even delicious, but modern diners at least are not likely to find it worth selling their birthrights for.)

It was in Midian that God spoke to Moses from a burning bush and instructed him to lead the children of Israel out of their bondage in Egypt. Moses' stern pleas to Pharaoh, their rejection, the plagues, and the final grudging permission for the Exodus followed—and so began the forty years of wandering in the Wilderness.

The children of Israel quickly began to long for the foods they had known: "We remember the fish, which we did eat in Egypt freely: the cucumbers, and the melons, and the leeks, and the onions, and the garlic" (Numbers 11:5). They complained that they had nothing but manna to sustain them. Exodus 13:31 says: "And the house of Israel called the name thereof Manna; and it was like coriander seed, white; and the taste was like wafers made with honey." Botanists and Bible historians continue to try to find a logical explanation for the appearance of "angels' food." Monks at St. Catherine's have a traditional explanation dating to the time of St. Anthony. The theory is that manna was formed from the secretion of insects on the tamarisk trees, which grow today in the southern Negev, the Arabbah Valley and in the wadis of the Sinai, close to the mountain where Moses received the Ten Commandments. This is neither available to American consumers, nor likely to be attractive to them, and the "manna" recipe we offer at least follows the description of the taste, being "wafers made with honey." The rest of Menu III is more abundant than that enjoyed by the Israelites in their wanderings; but the ingredients were and are found in various places in the Sinai and Negev deserts.

Lack of water also troubled the wanderers. Their grumblings were constant, especially in the wilderness of Zin. "And whereupon have ye made us to come up out of Egypt, to bring us in unto this evil place? it is no place of seed, or of figs, or of vines or of pomegranates; neither is there any water to drink" (Numbers 20:5). Kadesh was their residence at this time and it was here while suffering from thirst that "... Moses lifted up his hand and with his rod smote the rock twice: and the water came out abundantly, and the congregation drank, and their beasts also" (Numbers 20:11). Today, the remote Kadesh Barnea suddenly appears to the traveler, lush with date palms and olive groves fed by a steady stream of fresh water flowing through green grass.

When, after forty years of wandering in the desert, Moses neared the Promised Land, he knew he would never live to enjoy it—that the turbulent people he had led would inherit "the good land, a land of brooks of water, of fountains and depths that spring out of valleys and hills; a land of wheat and barley, and vines and fig trees, and pomegranates; a land of olive oil and honey; a land wherein thou shalt eat bread without scarceness, thou shalt not lack any thing" (Deuteronomy 8:7-9).

Menu IV reflects the abundance of that land and one fulfillment of its promise.

I

Moses in Pharaoh's Palace

CREAM OF ALMOND SOUP

1 quart chicken broth
¾ cup chopped blanched almonds
1 onion, chopped
1 cup chopped celery
3 tablespoons butter
3 tablespoons flour
1 cup cream
½ teaspoon almond extract
Salt, white pepper to taste

Combine broth, almonds, onion and celery; simmer 20 minutes. Place in a blender, cover and whirl until smooth. In a heavy saucepan, melt butter, add flour and cook until bubbling. Add broth and cook, stirring, until thickened. Add cream and seasonings; heat to boiling point. Serve immediately.

Note: This soup may also be served cold.

Makes 6 to 8 servings.

RED SEA SCALLOPS IN SHELLS

½ cup water
¼ cup lemon juice
1 bay leaf
4 to 5 peppercorns
4 to 5 parsley sprigs
A few celery tops
2 cups scallops
Heavy cream
3 tablespoons butter
3 tablespoons flour
Salt, pepper and Tabasco sauce to taste
Buttered bread crumbs

To prepare a court bouillon, combine water, lemon juice, bay leaf, peppercorns, parsley and celery tops in a heavy skillet. Simmer 15 minutes, then strain. Return to skillet; add scallops and simmer only until scallops are opaque (do not overcook) . Remove scallops and set aside. Measure broth and add enough cream to make 1½ cups.

In a saucepan, melt butter; add flour and cook, stirring until bubbling. Add broth-cream mixture all at once, and cook, stirring, until smooth and thick. Season to taste. Add scallops and pour into 4 individual shells or au gratin dishes. Sprinkle generously with buttered bread crumbs. Bake at 425 degrees for 10 minutes. Serve immediately.

Makes 4 servings.

GREEN BEANS VINAIGRETTE

1½ pounds fresh string beans
2½ quarts boiling salted water
2½ tablespoons Basic Salad Dressing
Chopped parsley
Chopped red onion

Snip off ends of beans, but leave them whole. Drop into rapidly boiling water and cook until barely tender, about 6 to 7 minutes. Drain at once and refresh by running cold water over them. Drain thoroughly. Arrange beans neatly on serving plate; chill. When ready to serve, spoon dressing over beans and sprinkle with chopped parsley and onion.

Makes 6 to 8 servings.

FAYYUM RICE
(Chutney Rice)

6 cups cooked rice
1 cup chutney
1 cup cream, whipped
1 teaspoon dry mustard
Salt, pepper and cumin

Combine rice and chutney; toss to mix thoroughly. Place in a shallow baking dish. Flavor cream with mustard, salt, pepper and cumin to taste. Pour over rice. Bake at 450 degrees for 10 minutes. Glaze top under the broiler and serve at once.

Makes 6 to 8 servings.

PICKLED MELON OF THE NILE
(Cantaloupe Pickle)

2 cups white vinegar
1¾ cups brown sugar, firmly packed
8 whole cloves
3 cinnamon sticks
½ teaspoon mace
3 cups firm, ripe cantaloupe, cut in cubes

Combine all ingredients except the melon and bring to a boil. Peel melon, removing green outer flesh, membranes and seeds. Cut the fruit into attractive shapes. Add melon pieces to the boiling liquid; reduce heat and simmer until tender and almost transparent. Using a slotted spoon, remove fruit and place in sterile hot jars. Pour syrup over fruit and seal while hot. A delightful addition to cold meat dishes.

Makes 1 quart.

LEMON CAKE PUDDING

1½ cups sugar
3 tablespoons flour
2 tablespoons softened butter
4 eggs, separated
1½ cups milk
1 tablespoon grated lemon peel
Juice of 2 lemons
Pinch of salt

Combine sugar and flour. Cream butter and add sugar-flour mixture, blending until smooth. Add egg yolks, 1 at a time, beating well after each addition. Add milk gradually, then the seasonings. Beat egg whites until stiff and fold into yolk mixture. Pour into a well-buttered 9-inch square cake pan and bake at 325 degrees for 40 minutes, or until top is golden and firm. The pudding will separate, forming a custard on the bottom and a cake texture on top.

Makes a 9-inch cake.

II

Moses in the Land of Goshen

PATRIARCHAL POTTAGE

2 cups split red lentils
2 quarts chicken broth
1 medium-sized onion
4 tablespoons butter
2 garlic cloves, minced
2 tablespoons ground cumin
Salt to taste
Freshly ground pepper
Lemon slices

Wash lentils in a sieve or colander under cold running water until draining water is clear. In a heavy soup kettle, heat broth. Chop onion coarsely, then sauté lightly in butter. Add lentils to broth and simmer 30 minutes or until beans are tender. Add onions and garlic; continue cooking 15 minutes. Put soup through a food mill, coarse sieve or blender, until smooth. Add seasonings. Serve garnished with lemon slices.

Makes 6 to 8 servings.

GOSHEN MEAT LOAF

½ cup dried lentils
3 cups water
1 pound lean ground beef
½ teaspoon pepper
¼ teaspoon saffron
1 teaspoon salt
1 egg
1 small onion, minced
1 teaspoon lemon juice
2 hard-cooked eggs
6 cooked prunes

Cook lentils in boiling water until tender (about 30 minutes). Mash them well and add to ground beef with all seasonings, egg, minced onion and lemon juice. Mix well. Divide into two parts. In center of each, place a peeled whole egg and 3 prunes. Surround these with the meat mixture, forming two small loaves. Bake at 350 degrees 40 minutes. Serve hot or cold.

Makes 6 to 8 servings.

CELERY ROOT PUREE

2 pounds celery root
2 pounds potatoes (substitute for ancient thickening agent)
4 tablespoons butter
Salt and white pepper to taste
Cream
2 hard-cooked eggs

Peel celery root and potatoes, cut into small dice. Cook in boiling salted water until tender (about 15 to 20 minutes).

Drain vegetables and whirl in a blender, or put through a food mill. Add butter, salt, pepper and enough cream to make a smooth puree. Garnish with sliced hard-cooked egg.

Makes 6 to 8 servings.

SCULPTURED BREAD DOUGH

1 cup chicken bouillon
1 cup hot water
2 tablespoons butter
2 tablespoons sugar
1½ teaspoons salt
1 package active dry yeast
¼ cup warm water
3 cups rice flour
2 cups unbleached flour

Heat bouillon and hot water in a saucepan to the boiling point. Add butter, sugar and salt. Cool to lukewarm. Dissolve yeast in the warm water. Combine liquids with yeast and rice flour; mix well. Add enough unbleached flour to make a soft dough. Turn out onto a floured surface and knead until dough is smooth and elastic. Place in a greased bowl, cover with a damp towel and allow to rise until doubled in bulk, about 1 hour. Punch down and knead thoroughly. Dough is then ready to form into coils or other desired shapes.

COILED SNAIL ROLLS

Break off a ball of dough about 2 inches in diameter and roll on floured surface to make a rope about 24 inches long and ½ inch thick. Starting at the center, form a coil, being careful not to stretch the dough. Place on greased baking sheet and allow to rise 15 minutes. Bake at 375 degrees 8 to 15 minutes or until done. Baking time depends on size of coil.

Makes about 3 dozen coiled rolls.

CAROB DELIGHT

1 cup sugar
1½ tablespoons cornstarch
Dash of salt
1 cup water
1 tablespoon butter
1 egg, slightly beaten
½ cup milk
3 tablespoons carob powder
1 teaspoon almond extract
1 cup cream, whipped

Combine sugar, cornstarch and salt with water in a heavy saucepan. Cook over medium heat until mixture thickens. Add butter and mix thoroughly. Allow to cool slightly, then add the egg. Cool the mixture, then add the milk and carob powder. Combine almond extract with whipped cream and fold in. Pile lightly into a serving dish and chill thoroughly before serving.

Makes 6 to 8 servings.

III

Moses in the Wilderness of Sinai

SINAI QUAIL WITH CHERRIES

6 quail or other small game birds
4 tablespoons butter
1¼ cup veal or chicken stock
1 can (30 ounces) sour cherries
Salt and pepper to taste
1 tablespoon currant jelly

Split the quail and brown quickly on all sides in butter. Place in a casserole. Drain cherries and reserve the juice. Combine stock, and reserved cherry juice. Pour over birds and simmer, covered, on top of stove or bake at 325 degrees, covered, 20 minutes or until tender. Drain off sauce and place in a saucepan. Heat to boiling and cook until sauce is reduced in half. Add currant jelly and cherries, season with salt and pepper. Pour over birds and serve with the cherries.

Makes 6 servings.

CABBAGE IN SOUR CREAM

4 tablespoons butter
1 medium head cabbage, shredded
Salt and freshly ground pepper to taste
2 tablespoons cider vinegar
1 tablespoon sugar
1 egg, slightly beaten
1 cup sour cream

Melt butter in a large skillet. Add cabbage and sauté lightly, stirring well. Sprinkle with salt, pepper, vinegar and sugar. Mix thoroughly. Combine egg and sour cream.

Reduce heat to very low. Pour egg mixture over cabbage, tossing lightly to cover the cabbage well. Do not boil. Re-season to taste and serve immediately.

Makes 6 to 8 servings.

BARLEY WITH ALMONDS

4 tablespoons butter
1 cup barley
½ cup blanched shredded almonds
3 cups beef or chicken broth
Salt and pepper

Melt butter in a large heavy skillet. Add barley and almonds. Toss to coat thoroughly. Remove to a casserole and add the broth. Cover and bake at 350 degrees for 45 minutes, stirring occasionally and adding water if the barley dries out too much. Uncover and cook 20 minutes longer or until barley is fluffy and tender. Season to taste with salt and pepper.

Makes 6 to 8 servings.

BITTER HERB SALAD WITH WILDERNESS SALAD DRESSING

1 full bunch chicory
1 bunch radishes
2 to 3 heads endive
¼ cup Wilderness Salad Dressing (recipe follows)

Carefully wash chicory, discarding bruised or torn leaves and hard white base of leaves. Tear into bite-sized pieces, wrap in a towel to dry and chill thoroughly. Wash radishes and remove stems and root ends. Slice thinly and soak in salted water for 15 minutes. Drain thoroughly. Remove center core of endives and slice into thin rounds. When ready to serve, place chicory in a salad bowl. Sprinkle on the radishes and endive. Drizzle dressing over all and toss lightly. Serve immediately.

Makes 6 to 8 servings.

WILDERNESS SALAD DRESSING

- ¼ cup honey
- ½ cup olive oil
- ¼ cup cider vinegar
- ¼ teaspoon cumin
- ⅛ teaspoon coriander
- ¼ teaspoon dill weed
- 1 teaspoon anise seed
- Salt to taste

Combine all ingredients in a jar or bottle and shake vigorously. Or whirl in a blender, if desired.

Makes about 1 cup dressing.

MANNA

- ½ cup butter
- 1 cup sugar
- 2 eggs
- 2 tablespoons honey
- ¼ teaspoon salt
- ½ teaspoon vanilla
- 1½ teaspoons baking powder
- 2 cups flour
- Coriander seeds

Cream butter, adding sugar gradually, until light and pale. Add eggs and beat thoroughly. Add honey, salt and vanilla. Combine baking powder with flour and add to butter mixture. Drop by half teaspoons onto a buttered cookie sheet. Garnish each cookie with 3 coriander seeds. Bake at 400 degrees 8 minutes or until done. Cool on wire racks.

Makes about 6 dozen cookies.

IV
The Promised Land

BUTTERFLY LEG OF LAMB

1 leg of lamb (5 to 6 pounds)
½ cup well-flavored mustard
2 tablespoons cider vinegar
2 tablespoons olive oil
1 teaspoon rosemary
2 teaspoons fresh chopped ginger root *or* ½ teaspoon ground ginger

Have butcher bone and split leg of lamb. When spread out, it will roughly resemble a butterfly—hence the name. Combine remaining ingredients and brush both sides of lamb. Allow to stand at room temperature at least 1 hour. Broil 15 to 18 minutes on each side, according to size of lamb leg. Do not overcook. Meat should be pink in center. Slice as a steak.

Makes 6 servings.

BROAD BEAN CASSEROLE

3 cups fresh *or* frozen lima beans
2 tablespoons butter
3 tablespoons chopped onions
Salt and freshly ground pepper
½ cup grated hard cheese
½ cup buttered bread crumbs

Cook fresh beans in small amount boiling salted water, covered, 20 or 30 minutes or until tender. If frozen, cook according to package directions. Drain thoroughly. In a heavy skillet, melt butter and sauté onion until limp. Add beans and toss to combine. Place in a casserole. Season to taste with salt and pepper. Sprinkle top with cheese and bread crumbs. Bake at 350 degrees 30 minutes.

Makes 6 to 8 servings.

FRUIT SALAD WITH PROMISED LAND SALAD DRESSING

1 cup watermelon balls
1 cup honeydew or cantaloupe balls
1 cup seedless grapes, halved
1 cup black grapes, halved
6 to 8 fresh figs
Salad greens
Promised Land Salad Dressing (recipe follows)

Using a melon scoop, cut melons into small balls. Prepare grapes, removing seeds and stems. Slice banana into strips and, if desired, sprinkle with lemon juice. Peel figs and slice carefully. Arrange salad greens on a large, flat platter.

Place a small bowl of Promised Land Salad Dressing in the center and arrange fruits attractively around it. Chill until ready to serve.

Makes 6 to 8 servings.

PROMISED LAND SALAD DRESSING

½ cup olive oil
1 teaspoon prepared mustard
¼ cup cider vinegar
1 tablespoon honey
¼ teaspoon whole sesame seed
⅛ teaspoon whole cumin seed
¼ teaspoon whole coriander seed
⅛ teaspoon grated garlic
½ teaspoon salt
½ teaspoon dried rue
Freshly ground black pepper

Add oil to mustard and blend well. Add other ingredients. Place in a jar or bottle and shake well before using.

Makes about ¾ cup dressing.

BEATEN BISCUITS

3 cups flour
1 teaspoon salt
1 teaspoon sugar
5 tablespoons butter
1 cup cold water (approximately)

Mix dry ingredients with the butter and combine until the consistency of meal. Add enough water to make a stiff dough. Knead thoroughly until dough is elastic and very smooth (about 5 minutes). Roll out on a lightly floured board to ½-inch thickness; cut with a biscuit cutter. Prick tops with a fork. Bake on a cookie sheet at 325 degrees for 30 minutes. Serve hot.

Makes about 3 dozen (2½-inch) biscuits.

CHEESE TORTE

½ cup butter
1 cup sugar
6 eggs, separated
½ cup (4 ounces) cottage cheese
½ teaspoon salt
Grated rind and juice of 1 lemon
½ cup ground almonds
Confectioners' sugar

Cream butter, adding sugar gradually. Add egg yolks one at a time, beating well, after each addition. Press cheese through a strainer and add to the butter mixture. Add lemon rind and juice. Beat egg whites with salt until stiff. Fold carefully into batter, adding ground almonds at same time. Pour batter into a well-buttered and floured 9-inch spring-form pan. Bake at 350 degrees 50 to 60 minutes or until top is firm when lightly pressed with finger. Dust with confectioners' sugar.

Makes a 9-inch torte.

CHAPTER THREE

DAVID

"And when David was a little past the top of the hill, behold Ziba the servant of Mephibosheth met him, with a couple of asses saddled and upon them two hundred loaves of bread, and an hundred bunches of raisins, and an hundred of summer fruits . . . and the bread and summer fruit for the young men to eat . . ." (II Samuel 16:2, 3).

Menus

I

Young David in Judah

BEEF STEW ENGEDI

YOGURT

SKILLET BREAD

PEAS WITH SCALLIONS

DATE NUT TORTE

LOAVES & FISHES

II

The Shepherd King

EGGS POACHED IN BROTH

LAMB ABIGAIL

KOUSA MASHI

JUDEAN FRUIT ROLL

III

David in Jerusalem

DEVILED WALNUTS

SWEET BUTTERED FISH

CANTALOUPE AND CUCUMBER SALAD

RYE BREAD

PLUM PIE

IV

David, Sweet Psalmist in Israel

FALAFEL

TABOON CHICKEN

KINNERET VEGETABLE

WALNUT PRALINES

DAVID

To be anointed as a king by a prophet of the Lord while the tyrant who considers himself king still holds the throne is never a very comfortable set of circumstances, nor a healthy one. David, son of Jesse, understood this very well, and fled into the hilly country around Engedi to avoid the wrath of King Saul. We can hope that his life in exile was sustained by such nourishing fare, then locally obtainable, as given in our Menu I—the Beef Stew Engedi is well suited to hiding out, being simply prepared and hearty. (For such dishes as this *leben,* crusty yogurt, was used; its preparation is quite complicated, and we have substituted an easier but tasty version in our recipe.) When eating his peas with scallions, David might also have enjoyed the reflection that the onion-like herb takes its name from Ashkelon, one of the cities of the Philistines, whose champion Goliath he had slain.

Sustenance was not always easily come by; and to feed his followers, David levied a toll against landholders whose flocks he protected against bandits. When he sent ten of his men to Nabal, a prosperous but obdurate man, asking for whatever food he could spare in return for protection, Nabal refused. However, Abigail, Nabal's wife, "a woman of good understanding, and of a beautiful countenance" (I Samuel 25:3) recognized the consequences of such a refusal. She made haste to David and "took two hundred loaves and two bottles of wine, and five sheep ready dressed, and five measures of parched corn, and an hundred clusters of raisins, and two hundred cakes of figs," (I Samuel 25:18) thus averting the wrath of David from her husband and household. She also taught David one of the wisest lessons of his life, which he acknowledged saying, ". . . blessed be thy advice, and blessed be thou, which hast kept me this day from coming to shed blood, and from avenging myself with mine own hand" (I Samuel 25:33).

After the death of Nabal, David married Abigail. We have paid tribute to her with Lamb Abigail (Menu II), a dish seasoned with mint, an herb as old as David's own city. Such a generous portion of figs and grapes as Abigail presented to David might be deliciously combined in a Judean Fruit Ring (Menu II).

Toward the end of his long and difficult apprenticeship, still unreconciled with Saul, David offered his services as a mercenary to the Philistines. Waging war for Israel's enemies, defending himself against Saul, and hungry in lonely encampments and strange Philistine cities, David's prayer in the twenty-third Psalm becomes even more poignant: "Thou preparest a table before me in the presence of mine enemies . . . my cup runneth over."

After the death of Saul at Mount Gilboa, the already-anointed king set out to win the approval of all the tribes of Israel and unite them into a single nation. He moved his capital from Hebron to Jerusalem, rebuilding the city and strengthening its fortifications. His personal involvement in war diminished and his energies were spent in establishing a strong kingdom. I Chronicles 27:26-29 tells of his appointments of officials to develop his royal estates—the vineyards, the olive and fig trees, the cattle, and the sheep, had their own stewards: "All these were the rulers of the substance which was King David's" (I Chronicles 27:31). A man of strong appetites, David would have delighted in the abundance provided by his land, and in the varied dishes the royal cooks would make of it. Menus III and IV contain such dishes and indicate the prosperity and tranquility this strong ruler brought to Israel.

I

Young David in Judah

BEEF STEW ENGEDI

3 pounds boneless beef (chuck or round)
2 to 3 tablespoons olive oil
1 clove chopped garlic (optional)
3 tablespoons flour
3 cups beef broth
2 bay leaves
Salt and pepper to taste
12 small white onions
2 tablespoons butter
1 cup water
1 small turnip, diced (½ cup)
Chopped parsley
Yogurt (recipe follows)

Trim fat from beef and cut into bite-sized cubes. In a large heavy skillet, heat oil. Add garlic and cook 1 minute, then transfer to a casserole. In same skillet, quickly brown beef cubes on all sides, transferring them to the casserole as they are browned. Sprinkle flour into the pan and allow it to brown. Gradually add 1 cup of beef broth and stir to assimilate all bits of browned flour. Pour mixture over the beef. Add remaining broth, bay leaves, salt and pepper. Cover and simmer until meat is tender, about 45 minutes. Meanwhile, prepare onions. Drop them into boiling water for a moment to loosen the skins, then peel. With a sharp knife, make a cross in each stem end to prevent the onions from falling apart during the cooking. In a shallow pan, melt butter with water. Add onions and cook 8 to 10 minutes or until almost tender. About 20 minutes before stew is done, add onions with their cooking liquid and the turnip. If carrots are used, parboil them and add at the same time. Garnish with finely chopped parsley and serve with yogurt on the side.

Makes 6 to 8 servings.

YOGURT

1 quart milk
3 tablespoons commercial yogurt
1 pint cream (optional)

Bring milk to a boil then allow to cool. While still quite warm, combine with yogurt, beating with a whisk. Allow to stand at room temperature until mixture is of custard consistency. If a thicker product is desired, add cream to the hot milk, then stir in the yogurt.

This recipe will produce a thin custard-like product, in no way like commercial yogurt. In cold weather, it could take 48 hours to thicken.

Makes 6 to 8 servings.

SKILLET BREAD

¾ cup flour
¾ teaspoon salt
3 eggs
¾ cup milk
4 tablespoons butter
2 tablespoons sugar

Combine dry ingredients. Add eggs and milk and beat lightly. Heat oven to 425 degrees. Place butter in 12-inch heavy skillet and heat until very hot. Pour in batter and bake 15 minutes. Sprinkle with sugar and put back in oven until brown on top.

Makes 4 to 6 servings.

PEAS WITH SCALLIONS

6 scallions
2 tablespoons butter
2 packages (10 ounces each) frozen green peas
¾ cup chicken stock
Salt and freshly ground pepper

Slice scallions into small rounds. Melt butter in heavy skillet; add scallions and sauté until tender but not browned. Add peas and chicken stock. Cover and simmer until peas are tender, according to label directions. Season to taste.

Makes 6 to 8 servings.

DATE NUT TORTE

3 eggs, separated
1 cup sugar
3 tablespoons crushed graham cracker crumbs
1¼ teaspoons baking powder
1 cup chopped pitted dates
1 cup chopped walnuts
½ teaspoon grated orange rind
¼ teaspoon salt
1 cup cream, whipped

Beat egg yolks, adding sugar gradually. Combine crumbs with baking powder. Beat egg whites until stiff; fold into yolks carefully, while adding remaining ingredients except the cream. Bake in a greased 9-inch square pan at 325 degrees 40 minutes. Cool in pan, then cut into squares. Serve with whipped cream.

Makes a 9-inch torte.

II
The Shepherd King

EGGS POACHED IN BROTH

1 cup beef broth
1 small onion, minced
Pinch thyme
1 bay leaf
6 eggs
6 slices buttered toast
1 tablespoon butter
1 tablespoon flour
Salt and white pepper to taste
Chopped parsley (garnish)

Combine broth, onion, thyme and bay leaf; simmer 10 minutes. Poach eggs carefully in this liquid. With a slotted spoon, remove eggs and place on toast. Keep warm while making the sauce. Rub together flour and butter, making a smooth paste—this is called *buerre manie*. Add to the liquid and cook, stirring constantly, until mixture thickens. Season with salt and white pepper; pour over eggs. Garnish with chopped parsley.

Makes 6 servings.

David

LAMB ABIGAIL
(Lamb Mint Ring)

4 teaspoons gelatin
¾ cup cider
¾ cup mild vinegar
¼ cup sugar
¾ cup finely chopped mint
½ cup stuffed green olives
2 cups cooked diced lamb
½ cup seedless raisins
Salt, pepper
Mayonnaise

Moisten gelatin with ¼ cup cider. Combine remaining ½ cup cider with vinegar and sugar. Heat until sugar dissolves. Add softened gelatin and mix thoroughly. Allow to cool. Add chopped mint. Slice stuffed olives and place in bottom of a 6-cup ring mold. Spoon enough of the mint mixture over them to cover, but not to float. Allow to congeal in refrigerator. Add diced lamb and raisins to mint mixture; mix well, then pour into prepared mold. Allow to chill several hours or until firm.

To unmold, set mold in hot water for a moment, loosen edges and invert onto a serving plate. Garnish with lettuce, mint and olives, if desired. Serve with well-flavored mayonnaise.

Makes 6 to 8 servings.

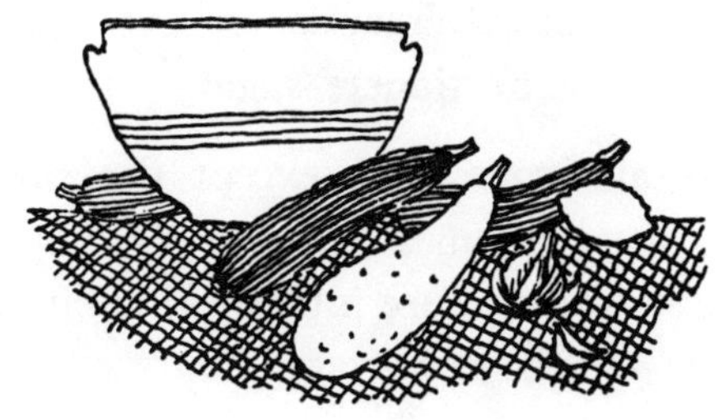

KOUSA MAHSHI

(Zucchini sauté)

⅓ cup olive oil
2 large mild onions, coarsely chopped
1 clove garlic, minced
3 zucchini, coarsely chopped
1 yellow squash, coarsely chopped
Salt and pepper to taste
A few fresh basil leaves, chopped, *or* 1 teaspoon dried
Juice of 1 lemon

Heat oil in a heavy skillet. Add onion and garlic; cook until limp. Add zucchini and squash. Season with salt, pepper, basil and lemon juice. Cook, stirring often, about 15 minutes. Do not overcook, as vegetables should be crisp. This may be served hot or cold as a salad.

Makes 6 to 8 servings.

JUDEAN FRUIT ROLL

1 pound dried pitted dates
1 pound seedless raisins
1 pound dried figs
1 pound walnuts
½ pound almonds
Confectioners' sugar

Combine all ingredients except the sugar and grind with the fine blade of a meat chopper, or chop very fine with a sharp knife. Form mixture into a roll about 2 inches in diameter. Allow to dry for several hours or overnight. Slice into thin rounds and dust generously with confectioners' sugar.

Makes 6 to 8 servings.

III

David in Jerusalem

DEVILED WALNUTS

1 tablespoon butter
2 cups walnut halves
2 tablespoons Worcestershire *or* **other hot sauce**
Dash cayenne pepper
1 teaspoon coarse salt

Melt butter in large skillet. Add nuts and toss to coat well. Add hot sauce and cayenne pepper. Mix well. Transfer to a shallow baking dish. Bake at 325 degrees for 20 minutes, stirring often. Sprinkle with salt and shake to coat nuts. Allow to cool completely before storing.

Makes 2 cups.

SWEET BUTTERED FISH

6 small fish fillets
4 tablespoons butter
4 tablespoons flour
1 cup clam juice
1 egg yolk, slightly beaten
½ cup cream
2 shallots, minced
Salt and white pepper to taste
1 cup seafood (such as crabmeat *or* small cooked shrimp)

Butter 6 rectangles of foil or parchment paper large enough to enfold fish fillets. Place a fillet on each rectangle. In a heavy saucepan, melt butter; add flour; then cook until bubbling and golden. Gradually add clam juice; cook, stirring constantly, until sauce is thick and smooth. Combine the egg yolk and cream; add to the sauce and stir over low heat until smooth and thickened. Season with shallots, salt and pepper. Place crabmeat or shrimp on each fillet and cover with sauce. Carefully fold up each packet. Place in a jelly roll pan and bake at 375 degrees for 20 minutes.

Makes 6 servings.

CANTALOUPE AND CUCUMBER SALAD

2 ripe cantaloupes
½ cup Basic Salad Dressing
1 large cucumber
1 teaspoon salt
½ cup sour cream
White pepper to taste
Dash of powdered ginger (optional)
Salad greens

Peel, seed and dice cantaloupe; marinate in French dressing. Peel and thinly slice the cucumber. Sprinkle with salt and allow to stand 30 minutes. Rinse with cold water and drain thoroughly. Combine cucumber and melon with sour cream. Season with salt, white pepper and ginger. Serve on crisp salad greens.

Makes 6 to 8 servings.

RYE BREAD

3 packages active dry yeast
2 cups lukewarm water
2 teaspoons salt
2 tablespoons oil
3½ cups all-purpose flour
2 cups dark rye flour
Caraway seed (optional)
2 tablespoons cornmeal (modern substitute for wild emmer)

Dissolve yeast in lukewarm water and let stand 5 minutes or until mixture starts to bubble. Add salt, oil and 2 cups all-purpose flour. Beat until smooth. Add rye flour and continue beating until dough is elastic and smooth. This may be done with an electric beater or kneaded by hand. Work in enough additional all-purpose flour to make a soft but firm dough. Cover with a damp towel and let rest 10 minutes. Knead on a floured board until dough is smooth. Place in a greased bowl, cover with a damp towel and allow to rise until double in bulk, about 1 hour. Punch down and allow to rise again. Divide dough in half and form into round loaves. Sprinkle with caraway seed, if desired. Place on heavy baking sheets, dusted with cornmeal. Allow to rise until double in bulk, about 1 hour. Bake at 375 degrees 45 minutes or until bread is nicely browned and sounds hollow when thumped on the bottom. Cool on wire racks.

Makes 2 round loaves.

PLUM PIE

1 cup sugar
¼ cup flour
¼ cup soft butter
3 eggs
1 teaspoon grated lemon peel
3 cups fresh prune plums
Butter Crust (recipe follows)

Mix sugar and flour, then work in butter to make a smooth mixture. Add eggs and lemon peel; combine well. Cut plums in half and remove pits. Place plums, cut side up, on pastry shell. Pour sugar mixture over plums and bake at 350 degrees for 45 to 50 minutes.

Note: Any desired crust may be substituted, but the rich butter crust is excellent with this filling.

BUTTER CRUST

1¼ cups flour
½ teaspoon salt
4 tablespoons butter (cool)
3 tablespoons vegetable shortening
2 to 3 tablespoons ice water

Place flour and salt in a large bowl. Break butter into pieces and add to the flour with the vegetable shortening. Crumble butter and shortening into the flour, using finger tips or a pastry blender. When well combined, sprinkle ice water over ingredients and mix quickly. Form into a ball, roll in wax paper and chill 30 minutes. Roll out pastry between 2 sheets of wax paper into a circle about 2 inches larger than pie plate and ⅛ inch thick. Peel off top sheet of paper. Transfer pastry on bottom sheet of paper to pie plate, pastry side down. Gently peel off paper and ease pastry into bottom and sides of plates. Make a decorative edge, then fill and bake as directed in Plum Pie recipe.

Makes a 9-inch pie shell.

IV

David, Sweet Psalmist in Israel

FALAFEL

(Chick-Pea Croquettes)

2 cups canned or cooked chick-peas, drained thoroughly
½ cup water
1 tablespoon flour
1 egg
1 slice bread, crumbled
3 cloves garlic, minced
½ teaspoon soda
¾ teaspoon salt (or to taste)
¼ teaspoon *each* cumin, basil, pepper and marjoram
Flour for dredging
Deep fat for frying
2 tablespoons chopped mint (garnish)

Grind chick-peas through the coarse blade of a meat grinder or whirl in a blender. Combine with water, flour, egg, bread, garlic and soda. Add salt to taste and spices. Form into small balls and dredge with flour. Fry quickly in deep fat until golden brown. Drain on paper towels. Serve hot sprinkled with mint.

Makes 6 to 8 servings.

TABOON CHICKEN

8 large onions, finely chopped
3 tablespoons olive oil
2 tablespoons Spice of Hebron
5 tablespoons pine nuts
1 large roasting chicken (about 5 pounds)
Salt
2 discs Pita Bread
2 cups hot cooked rice (fluffy white or saffron)

Cook onions in 2 tablespoons olive oil until transparent but still slightly firm. Strain to remove as much oil and liquid as possible. Saute pine nuts in remaining 1 tablespoon oil. Remove from oil with slotted spoon and drain on paper towel. Mix spice and 4 tablespoons pine nuts with onions. Sprinkle chicken cavity and rub outside skin with salt. Fill chicken cavity with onion mixture leaving 3/4 cup for garnish. Bake covered with foil at 350 degrees 1 1/2 hours. Remove foil and continue baking 1/2 hour or until tender, basting frequently with pan juices. When chicken is done, place Pita bread on a heated serving platter. Transfer chicken to another heated platter; spoon pan juices over bread. Spoon rice on bread, then place chicken on rice. Sprinkle top of chicken with remaining onion mixture and pine nuts. Keep warm in oven until ready to serve.

Makes 6 to 8 servings.

KINNERET VEGETABLES
(Squash Sauté)

2 crookneck squash
2 medium zucchini
2 patty-pan squash
Water
Salt and pepper
Dash of cumin
Chopped fresh dill
1 cup chopped almonds or pine nuts
4 tablespoons butter, melted

Wash squash and remove stem ends but do not peel. Cut into ½-inch slices. Place in a large saucepan and pour boiling water over to about a depth of 1 inch. Cover and simmer until vegetables are tender but not mushy, about 15 minutes. Drain thoroughly. Arrange half the squash in a greased shallow baking dish. Add salt, pepper, cumin and dill to taste. Sprinkle on half the nuts. Repeat with remaining squash and nuts. Drizzle melted butter over all and bake at 375 degrees 15 minutes or until heated through.

Makes 6 to 8 servings.

WALNUT PRALINES

3 cups brown sugar
1 cup cream
½ cup butter
Peel of 1 orange
2 cups walnut halves
Dash of salt

Combine brown sugar, cream, butter and orange peel in a heavy saucepan. Cook until mixture forms a soft ball when a teaspoonful is dropped into cold water. Remove orange peel and add walnuts and salt. Beat well and drop in small quantities onto buttered wax paper.

Makes about 16 (2½-inch) pralines.

CHAPTER FOUR

SOLOMON

"And Solomon's provision for one day was thirty measures of fine flour and three-score measures of meal, ten fat oxen and twenty oxen out of the pastures, and an hundred sheep, besides harts, and roebucks, and fallow deer, and fatted fowl" (I Kings 4:22, 23).

Menus

I

Solomon, the Anointed King

CORONATION FISH

WITH

TARATOOR

BRAISED LEEKS OF GIBEON

EN-ROGEL SALAD

APRICOT TRIFLE

II

Solomon on the Temple Mount

ROYAL GARDEN CANAPÉ

HESHBON FILLETS

GREEN AND GOLD SALAD

HERB BISCUITS

KIDRON MELON MOUSSE

LIME WAFERS

III

King Solomon and Queen of Sheba Banquet

POMEGRANATE NECTAR

INDIAN CHICKEN CURRY

CONDIMENTS FOR CURRIES

SAFFRON RICE

LEMON CHUTNEY

PEACH CHUTNEY

OPHIR BAKED MELON

IV

Solomon in His Royal Cities

EGYPTIAN CELERY SOUP

LAMB WITH DILL

TARSHISH FRITTERS

SPINACH ROLL MEGIDDO

DATE ORANGE CAKE

SOLOMON

"So King Solomon exceeded all the kings of the earth for riches and for wisdom" (I Kings 10:23). Under his reign, Israel became a great center of culture and trade. Solomon's ships established commercial trade routes to Phoenicia, Egypt, Sardinia and perhaps Spain; on land, camel caravans traveled to Arabia. Wood, metals, cloth and various luxuries flowed into the country in exchange for corn, oil, wine, honey, fruit and aromatics. He introduced many new plants and foods to Israel and imported exotic spices for the royal kitchen.

Solomon's coronation had been hasty, but the celebrations which followed were surely appropriately grand for the king who is even today thought of "in all his glory" (Luke 12:27). The haste was occasioned by Adonijah, Solomon's eldest brother, who gathered military and religious followers together as King David, their father, was dying, and had himself proclaimed king.

While Adonijah was preparing his coronation feast at En-rogel, Solomon's mother, Bathsheba, and the prophet Nathan persuaded David to name Solomon as his heir. Protected by a faithful guard of mighty men, Solomon was anointed king at the Spring of Gihon, near En-rogel. When Adonijah's supporters heard the trumpet blast announcing Solomon's coronation, they deserted the self-crowned king and simply faded away. Or perhaps some of them even attended the banquet given for Solomon. Coronation fish with taratoor served with leeks and other vegetables would have been a royal dish, yet simple and quick enough to prepare for the impromptu celebration when Solomon returned from Gihon.

Solomon may have used the fish pools at Heshbon to provide fresh fish for his royal table. The Song of Solomon refers to them (7:4): "thine eyes like the fishpools in Heshbon, by the gate of Bathrabbim." He also raised his own meat throughout the country and appointed district managers to send provisions to the palace according to a regular schedule. Solomon and his sumptuous court demanded rich fare for their table: "And Solomon's provision for one day was thirty measures of fine flour [about 335 bushels] and three-score measures of meal, ten fat oxen and twenty oxen out of the pastures, and an hundred sheep, besides harts, and roebuck, and fallow deer, and fatted fowl" (I Kings 4:22, 23).

Solomon's fame spread as an extraordinarily wise king, an able and astute diplomat and as the architect of fine buildings. Even the Queen of Sheba undertook a long and arduous journey to witness personally his prosperity. She traveled with her elegant retinue to Jerusalem bearing all manner of expensive gifts and the rare spices that would be used in curry dishes. The Bible does not indicate how they feasted during her stay, but Solomon must have outdone himself to surprise his glamorous visitor with superlative food.

As an architect it was Solomon's task to realize David's dream of building a temple where the Ark of the Lord would have an appropriate resting place. In addition to his magnificent palace in Jerusalem, he built three other royal cities with palaces at Megiddo, Gezer, and Hazor. All three have been excavated by archaeologists and indicate further Solomon's ultra-civilized life-style.

About fifty years ago a limestone plaque was uncovered at Gezer written by a schoolboy as an exercise. It dates from about the tenth century B.C., around Solomon's time, and provides us with a remarkable glimpse of a farmer's yearly schedule.

> "His two months are olive harvest;
> his two months are planting grain
> his two months are late planting
> his month is hoeing up of flax
> his month is harvest of barley;
> his month is harvest and festivity;
> his two months are vine-tending;
> his month is summer fruit."

Also at Gezer were found charred remains of fruit, nuts and cereals: wheat, barley, oats, beans, figs, grapes, pomegranates, olives, pistachio nuts, acorn and apricot seeds. The plump red pomegranate, the emblem of fertility, became a decorative theme in Solomon's household and on his furnishings. "And the chapiters upon the two pillars had pomegranates also above . . . and the pomegranates were two hundred in rows round about upon the other chapiter" (I Kings 7:20).

Now, if you plan a King Solomon dinner party do not hesitate to bring out the family heirlooms, especially the gold pieces—be authentic! "And all King Solomon's drinking vessels were of gold, and all the vessels . . . were of pure gold; none were of silver, it was nothing accounted of in the days of Solomon . . . once in three years came the navy of Tarshish bringing gold, and silver, ivory, and apes and peacocks" (I Kings 10:21, 22).

I

Solomon, the Anointed King

CORONATION FISH WITH TARATOOR

½ cup olive oil
1 cup finely chopped onion
1 cup seedless green grapes
1 cup walnuts, crushed
½ cup chopped parsley
3 tablespoons pomegranate seeds
3 teaspoons salt
Freshly ground black pepper
1 whole fish (3 to 4 pounds), such as striped bass, cleaned and with head and tail intact
1 recipe Taratoor (recipe follows)
1 lemon

Heat oil in a large skillet. Add onion and cook until transparent. Add grapes and walnuts and mix thoroughly. Remove from heat and add parsley and pomegranate seeds. Season mixture with salt and pepper. Stuff fish cavity lightly with the mixture, securing with small skewers.

Spread Taratoor evenly over surface of fish. Bake at 400 degrees for 40 to 50 minutes or until the fish flakes, when tested with a fork in the fleshiest part. Garnish with pomegranate seeds and thin lemon slices if desired.

Makes 6 to 8 servings.

TARATOOR

3 cloves garlic
1 cup tahini paste (sesame seed paste)
¾ cup cold water
½ cup fresh lemon juice
1 teaspoon salt (or to taste)

Crush garlic to a paste in a mortar or mince very finely. Add to tahini paste. Beat with a whisk, adding water and lemon juice to make a smooth sauce the consistency of mayonnaise. Salt to taste.

Makes about 2 cups sauce.

BRAISED LEEKS OF GIBEON

6 leeks
3 tablespoons butter
2 cups chicken broth
Salt and pepper to taste
Juice of 1 lemon
¼ cup chopped parsley

Soak leeks in cold water then wash thoroughly holding the leaves apart. Remove stems to top of white part and slice off root base. If leeks are very large, they may be cut in half lengthwise. Melt butter in a heavy shallow pan and brown leeks slightly. Add broth to cover and simmer very gently until leeks are tender, about 15 minutes. Remove to a heated serving dish. Increase heat and cook the broth until it is reduced to about ½ cup. Add seasonings and lemon juice; pour over the leeks. Serve immediately garnished with chopped parsley.

Note: The leeks may also be served cold. If so, use oil for browning instead of butter.

Makes 6 to 8 servings.

EN-ROGEL SALAD
(Chicory Salad)

1 large bunch chicory
1 can (8 ounces) Mandarin orange segments, drained
2 tablespoons grated coconut
¼ cup salad dressing

Carefully wash chicory, discarding bruised or brown leaves and hard white base of leaves. Tear into bite-sized pieces and dry thoroughly. When ready to serve, place chicory in a glass bowl and top with orange segments. Sprinkle with coconut and pour dressing over all. Toss lightly and serve at once.

Makes 6 to 8 servings.

APRICOT TRIFLE

2 eggs plus 1 yolk
⅓ cup sugar
1½ tablespoons flour
3 cups milk
Dash of salt
½ teaspoon almond extract
3 cups stale cake (approximately)
2 cups stewed apricots

In a heavy saucepan, combine eggs and yolk with sugar and flour. Add milk gradually to avoid lumping. Cook over medium heat, stirring constantly, until custard thickens. Season with salt and almond extract. Crumble a third of the cake into a serving dish. Add a third of the apricots, then some of the custard. Repeat until all ingredients have been used, ending with a layer of custard. Chill thoroughly.

Makes 6 to 8 servings.

II

Solomon on the Temple Mount

ROYAL GARDEN CANAPÉ

(Eggplant Hors d'oeuvre)

1 eggplant
1 tablespoon salt
3 tablespoons olive oil
1 clove garlic, minced fine
1 cup yogurt

Cut unpeeled eggplant into ½ inch slices. Sprinkle with salt and let stand 30 minutes. Rinse salt off and dry eggplant on paper towels. Sauté the slices in olive oil. Cut them in half and allow to drain and cool. Combine garlic and yogurt. Arrange eggplant on a serving dish in overlapping slices and spread yogurt over. Chill 1 hour or more before serving as a first course.

Makes 6 to 8 servings.

HESHBON FILLETS

3 packages (10 ounce each) frozen chopped spinach (substitute for purslane)
1 pint sour cream
3 tablespoons flour
Juice of 1 lemon
½ cup finely minced onion
2 teaspoons salt (or to taste)
Pepper and nutmeg to taste
6 to 8 flounder fillets
2 tablespoons butter

Cook spinach according to package directions and drain thoroughly. Place sour cream in a mixing bowl and add flour, lemon juice and onion. Season spinach with salt, pepper and nutmeg. Spread on surface of a shallow baking dish. Place fish on the spinach and spoon sour cream sauce over all. Melt butter and pour over top. Bake at 375 degrees 25 minutes or until fish flakes easily with a fork.

Makes 6 to 8 servings.

GREEN AND GOLD SALAD

½ cup mayonnaise
½ cup sour cream
2 tablespoons olive oil
1 tablespoon vinegar
½ teaspoon curry powder
Salt and Tabasco sauce to taste
½ cup chutney
1 cucumber, sliced
½ honeydew melon
1 can (8 ounce) Mandarin oranges
2 to 3 bananas
Lettuce

Combine mayonnaise, sour cream, olive oil, vinegar, seasonings and chutney in blender and whirl until smooth. Allow to chill 1 to 2 hours. Arrange cucumber and fruits on a bed of crisp lettuce. Serve with chilled sauce.

Makes 6 to 8 servings.

HERB BISCUITS

2 cups unsifted flour
1 teaspoon salt
4 teaspoons baking powder
4 tablespoons vegetable shortening
2 tablespoons finely chopped fresh herbs (rosemary, chives or basil)
¾ cup milk

Preheat oven to 425 degrees. Combine dry ingredients in a large bowl. Add shortening and herbs. Mix lightly with tips of fingers. Add milk and stir together quickly with a spoon. On a lightly floured surface, roll out dough to ⅓-inch thickness. Cut biscuits with a small cutter (1½ inch or smaller) and place on an ungreased cookie sheet. Brush biscuits with a small amount of milk and bake for 12 minutes or until delicately brown.

Makes about 4 dozen biscuits.

KIDRON MELON MOUSSE
(Cantaloupe Mousse)

2 cups mashed ripe cantaloupe
½ cup sugar (or to taste)
1 envelope gelatin
¼ cup cold water
1 teaspoon vanilla
Lemon or lime juice to taste
1 cup cream

Combine cantaloupe and sugar; heat until sugar is dissolved. Soften gelatin in cold water, then add to the warm fruit to dissolve. Add flavorings. Whip cream and fold into mixture. Chill thoroughly before serving.

Note: Honeydew or other flavorful melon may be substituted.

Makes 6 to 8 servings.

LIME WAFERS

1 cup butter or margarine
1½ cups sugar
1 egg
1 tablespoon lime juice
Grated rind of 1 lime
¼ teaspoon salt
1 teaspoon soda
½ cup buttermilk
4 cups flour
1 teaspoon baking powder

Cream butter or margarine, adding sugar gradually and beating until very light. Add egg and seasonings. Mix soda and buttermilk; add alternately to butter mixture with flour and baking powder. Form dough into 3 flat balls and chill for 3 to 4 hours. Roll dough out to 1/8 inch thickness and cut into desired shapes. Bake on greased cookie sheet at 350 degrees 10 to 12 minutes or until golden. Dust with sugar and cool on racks. Granulated sugar may be dusted on before baking for a glazed effect, if desired.

Makes about 5 dozen small cookies.

III

King Solomon and Queen of Sheba Banquet

POMEGRANATE NECTAR

1 cup grenadine syrup
1 cup orange juice
4 tablespoons lemon juice
4 cups ginger ale

Combine all ingredients and pour over shaved ice.

Note: Grenadine is made from the juice of pomegranate.

Makes 6 to 8 servings.

Solomon

INDIAN CHICKEN CURRY

3 tablespoons olive oil
1 large onion, chopped
2 tablespoons Curry Powder
Salt to taste
2 tablespoons flour
1 apple, peeled, cored and chopped
1½ cups rich chicken broth
3 cups cooked diced chicken
3 tablespoons chopped fresh mint

Melt oil in a heavy skillet. Add onion and cook until limp. Combine curry powder with salt and flour and sprinkle on onions; mix thoroughly. Add apple, then broth and cook until tender. Add chicken and mint. Correct seasoning. Serve with saffron rice and assorted condiments.

Note: Lamb or beef cubes or cooked seafood may be substituted for the chicken.

Makes 6 to 8 servings.

CURRY POWDER

6 teaspoons ground ginger
6 teaspoons ground coriander
3 teaspoons ground cardamom
¼ teaspoon *each* basil and cracked red pepper
2 teaspoons ground cloves
2 teaspoons ground cumin
3 teaspoons ground turmeric

Combine all spices and store in an airtight jar.

Makes 1 pint.

CONDIMENTS FOR CURRIES

1. *Raisins:* 1 cup raisins
¼ cup grape juice

Cover raisins with boiling water and let stand 15 minutes. Drain thoroughly. Add grape juice and soak for at least 1 hour before serving.

2. *Peanuts:* Partially crush shelled peanuts before serving.

3. *Chutney:* See index.

4. *Coconut:* This condiment is an essential for a curry. Fresh coconut should be used, if possible. To prepare a coconut, punch 2 holes in the top, invert and drain the liquid into a glass (this may be added to the curry sauce). Crack the coconut with a hammer. Place the pieces in a shallow pan and heat in a 300 degree oven for 10 minutes. This will loosen the rough outer shell, which may then be pried off with a knife. The inner skin must then be cut off and discarded. The white meat should be rinsed to remove any dark bits. Place it in a blender and whirl to produce fine grated coconut. This may be frozen for other uses as well.

5. *Broiled bananas:* Peel bananas and slice lengthwise. Sprinkle with lemon or lime juice. Dot with butter and sprinkle with brown sugar. Broil quickly. Do not overcook.

6. *Hard-cooked eggs:* Chop egg whites into small dice. Rub the yolks through a sieve. Serve in separate bowls for a variety of color and texture.

7. *Wilted Cucumbers:* See index.

Note: All condiments should be served in similar small bowls, with a spoon for each.

SAFFRON RICE

1 cup raw rice
4 tablespoons butter, melted
2 tablespoons chopped onion
2 cups chicken stock
¼ teaspoon saffron strands
Salt and pepper
Chopped parsley (garnish)

In a heavy skillet, coat rice with melted butter. Add onion and cook, stirring until onion is limp. Add stock. Crumble saffron into the mixture. Cover and simmer until rice is tender (about 20 minutes). Season to taste. Garnish with chopped parsley.

Makes 6 to 8 servings.

LEMON CHUTNEY

6 large lemons
1¾ cups sugar
¼ cup water
Dash of salt
½ cup white raisins
1 cup cider vinegar
2 cinnamon sticks
½ teaspoon whole allspice
½ teaspoon whole cloves
½ cup nuts (pistachios, if available)

Slice lemons as thinly as possible, discarding seeds and tough white parts. Combine all ingredients and cook over medium heat 15 minutes. Fill sterile hot jars and seal while hot.

Makes 2 pints.

PEACH CHUTNEY

1 pound grated peaches
½ cup water
½ cup vinegar
1 tablespoon fresh lime juice
½ tablespoon ground cloves
4 bay leaves
¼ cup chopped pitted dates
⅓ cup seedless raisins
1 teaspoon cayenne pepper
3 teaspoons salt
1 teaspoon cinnamon
½ teaspoon nutmeg
⅓ cup toasted slivered almonds
1 pound sugar
1 teaspoon cumin seed
1 teaspoon ground ginger
¼ cup chopped pistachio nuts

Combine all ingredients and cook until mixture thickens, about 30 minutes. Place in sterile hot jars and seal while hot.

Makes about 1½ pints.

OPHIR BAKED MELON

Select a firm ripe melon such as cantaloupe. Remove rind and seeds. Slice into serving pieces. Dot generously with butter, salt, pepper and lemon juice. Cover with buttered baking paper and bake at 350 degrees for 35 minutes. Serve hot, as a vegetable.

Makes 6 to 8 servings.

IV

Solomon in His Royal Cities

EGYPTIAN CELERY SOUP

1 tablespoon butter
1 small onion, chopped
2 cups chopped celery
1 tablespoon flour
4 cups rich chicken broth
1½ cups light cream
Salt and white pepper

Melt butter in a heavy skillet. Add onion and cook until limp. Add celery and toss to cover with butter. Sprinkle on flour and cook 1 to 2 minutes. Add 1 cup stock and mix thoroughly. Transfer to a saucepan and add remaining stock. Simmer soup 20 minutes or until celery is tender. Add cream and season to taste. Serve hot or cold.

Note: Soup may be pureed in a blender if desired.

Makes 6 to 8 servings.

LAMB WITH DILL

1 leg of lamb (4 to 5 pounds)
2 cloves garlic, chopped
½ cup chopped fresh dill or 1 tablespoon dried
½ cup lemon juice
½ cup water
½ cup mild vinegar
Salt to taste

Make small incisions in the lamb with a sharp paring knife. Insert bits of garlic. Rub surface of lamb with dill, pressing it into the meat. Place lamb in a baking pan and pour on liquids. Allow to marinate several hours, turning often. Bake at 325 degrees, allowing 15 to 18 minutes for each pound. Baste often with the pan juices. Sprinkle with salt during the last 15 minutes of cooking.

Makes 6 to 8 servings.

TARSHISH FRITTERS

2 packages artichoke hearts
3 egg yolks
1½ cups flour
1¼ cups milk
1 teaspoon baking powder
Salt and pepper to taste
Dash of nutmeg

Cook artichokes according to directions on package. Drain well. Beat egg yolks, adding flour and milk alternately to make a fairly thin batter. Season well, add baking powder and mix thoroughly. Dip artichoke hearts in batter and fry quickly in hot oil.

Makes 6 to 8 servings.

SPINACH ROLL MEGIDDO

3 packages (10 ounces each) frozen chopped spinach (substitute for purslane)
5 eggs, separated
6 tablespoons melted butter
Salt, pepper and nutmeg to taste

Cook spinach according to package directions. Drain thoroughly, Add egg yolks, melted butter and seasonings. Mix well. Beat egg whites until stiff, then fold carefully into spinach. Butter a jelly-roll pan, line with wax paper and butter again. Spread spinach mixture evenly into pan. Bake at 375 degrees for 15 minutes, or until spinach is dry to the touch. Turn out of pan and fill with any desired filling, such as scrambled eggs, creamed seafood or creamed chicken. Roll up, jelly-roll fashion, and return to oven to heat thoroughly.

Makes 6 to 8 servings.

DATE ORANGE CAKE

1 pound pitted dates
4 cups flour
1 cup butter
2 cups sugar
4 eggs, separated
½ teaspoon salt
1 teaspoon soda
1¼ cups buttermilk
2 cups coarsely chopped pecans or walnuts

Preheat oven to 325 degrees. Chop dates and mix with ⅓ cup flour to separate pieces. Cream butter, adding sugar gradually until light and lemon colored. Beat in egg yolks. Combine remaining 3⅔ cups flour with the salt. Combine soda with the buttermilk and add to the butter mixture alternately with the flour. When well combined, add nuts and dates. Beat egg whites until stiff and fold in. Bake in a large ungreased tube pan for 1¾ to 2 hours or until cake is delicately brown and firm.

TOPPING

2 cups sugar
1 cup orange juice concentrate
2 tablespoons grated orange rind

Mix all ingredients together and let mixture stand at room temperature. As soon as the cake is out of the oven, punch holes over the surface with a skewer. Pour topping mixture over cake, repeating until all the mixture is absorbed by the cake.

Note: This cake improves with age. Store in the refrigerator in an airtight container.

Makes a 9-inch cake.

From the New Testament

CHAPTER FIVE

CAESAR AUGUSTUS

"And it came to pass in those days, that there went out a decree from Caesar Augustus, that all the world should be taxed" (Luke 2:1).

Menu

TIBER FISH STEW

PAN BREAD

SPINACH CUSTARD

CAESAR GREENS

COMPOTE OF MELONS

CARDAMOM CAKES

CAESAR AUGUSTUS

The first ruler of Rome to be granted the title of Emperor, Augustus participated in the battles and plots that ushered in the age of comparative stability called the *Pax Romana,* during which Christianity arose and flourished. His greatest Biblical prominence comes from his efforts to achieve that stability—his decree that "all the world be taxed" (Luke 2:1), or rather that a general census be taken, a decree which brought Joseph and Mary to a stable in Bethlehem and made that little town forever sacred.

Augustus was held in high esteem by his people and regarded with respect and admiration by the governors of his provinces. A birthday inscription in 7 B.C. states that "everything was deteriorating and changing into misfortune, but he set it right and gave the whole world another appearance . . ." Herod the Great built the city of Caesarea in honor of Augustus and named his reconstructed city of Samaria "Sebaste," from the Greek name for Augustus.

Although Augustus believed in prosperity for his subjects, he was spartan in his own habits. He lived simply and was known for his modest taste in dress and the frugality of his meals. We have tried to reflect this in his menu.

TIBER FISH STEW

Bones, head and skin of any fish
6 cups water
1 onion, chopped
3 tablespoons butter
1 to 2 ribs celery, diced
2 potatoes
Salt and pepper to taste
1½ cups flaked cooked fish
Minced parsley (garnish)

Place fish bones, head and skin in a soup kettle with the water. Allow to simmer 30 minutes. Strain and discard fish scraps. Sauté onion in butter until limp. Add celery and cook briefly. Peel and dice potatoes, add to broth and simmer until tender. Add celery and onion; and simmer 15 minutes. Season well. Add flaked fish. Serve very hot. Garnish with parsley.

Makes 6 to 8 servings.

PAN BREAD

1 can (8½ ounces) cream-style corn
1 cup yellow cornmeal (similar to wild emmer)
2 eggs slightly beaten
⅓ cup vegetable oil
1 teaspoon salt
½ teaspoon soda
¾ cup milk
1 tablespoon butter
½ cup shredded sharp cheese

Combine corn, cornmeal, eggs, vegetable oil, salt, soda and milk. Add half the cheese. Melt butter in a 9-inch brownie pan and pour mixture in. Bake at 400 degrees 45 to 50 minutes. Serve hot. Sprinkle on remaining cheese.

Makes 6-8 servings.

SPINACH CUSTARD

2 packages (10 ounces each) frozen chopped spinach
4 slices white bread, crusts removed
½ pound sharp cheese, grated
2 eggs
1 cup milk
1 teaspoon dry mustard
Salt, pepper and Tabasco sauce to taste

Cook spinach according to package directions; drain thoroughly. Butter a casserole generously. Place 2 slices bread on bottom, then cover with half the spinach and half the cheese. Repeat, ending with cheese. Combine eggs, milk and seasonings; pour over all. Bake at 350 degrees 35 to 45 minutes or until set.

Makes 6 to 8 servings.

CAESAR GREENS

2 eggs
1 clove garlic
¾ cup olive oil
2 cups crisp croutons
2 bunches romaine lettuce
Salt and freshly ground pepper
Juice of 1 lemon
6 to 8 flat anchovies
½ cup grated Parmesan cheese

Boil eggs for exactly 1 minute and set aside. In a small bowl, crush garlic and pour oil over it. Make croutons, using some of this oil for frying. Tear lettuce into bite-sized pieces, discarding spines and tough parts. Place in a large salad bowl. Pour on ¼ cup oil, and add salt and pepper to taste; toss lightly until leaves are glossy. Break in the eggs, add lemon juice and toss again. Add anchovies, croutons and grated cheese. Toss and serve at once.

Note: To make croutons, remove crusts of bread and reserve for other uses. Cut bread into small cubes. Heat a small amount of oil in a heavy skillet and fry croutons, shaking the pan constantly, until bread is toasted brown and crisp on all sides. Drain on paper towels.

Makes 6 to 8 servings.

COMPOTE OF MELONS

1 honeydew melon
1 cantaloupe
¼ watermelon
Nutmeg
Lime juice
Fresh mint sprigs

Cut melons in half; remove seeds and membranes. Form into small balls with melon scoop and place in a serving bowl. Sprinkle with lime juice and freshly grated nutmeg. Garnish with sprigs of fresh mint.

Makes 6 to 8 servings.

CARDAMOM CAKES

⅓ cup butter
10 tablespoons sugar
2 eggs
1¾ to 2 cups flour
⅛ teaspoon salt
½ teaspoon crushed cardamom seeds
2 teaspoons baking powder

Cream butter, adding sugar gradually. Add eggs, one at a time, beating well after each addition. Add enough flour to make a firm dough. Mix salt, cardamom and baking powder with the last ¼ cup flour added. Chill dough 1 hour or longer. Roll out on a lightly floured surface. Dough should be rolled as thinly as possible. Cut into desired shapes and bake on an ungreased cookie sheet at 375 degrees for 10 minutes.

Makes about 5 dozen (1½-inch) cookies.

CHAPTER SIX

HEROD THE GREAT

"Now when Jesus was born in Bethlehem of Judaea in the days of Herod the king, behold . . ." (Matthew 2:1).

Menu

TYCHE SOUP

BRAISED DUCK

VALLEY OF ESCHOL ARTICHOKE

ALMOND POACHED PEARS

WITH

THICKENED CREAM

HEROD THE GREAT

In achieving stability, Augustus, like all rulers and politicians, had to recognize his obligations to those who helped him without too much regard to their characters or abilities. The wily, cruel, ambitious Herod, having jumped nimbly from side to side during Rome's civil wars, had wound up supporting Octavian, who later was granted the title of Augustus. Herod had to be granted something in return. What he got was the backing of Rome in asserting his power as King of Judea. He was thus enabled to rule for more than thirty years, to slaughter those who did or even might oppose him, including his wife Mariamne, the most beautiful woman of her time—and, virtually in passing, to order the precautionary Massacre of the Innocents.

Like many tyrants, past and present, Herod was a fanatic builder and a confirmed lover of luxury. His remarkable fortress-palace at Masada near the Dead Sea illustrates this. Built on a mountain 1,700 feet above sea level, it was described by the historian Josephus as "fortified by heaven and man against any enemy who might wage war against it." According to Josephus, "the wall of this palace was very high and strong, and had at its four corners towers sixty feet high . . . the furniture of the edifices, and of the cloisters, of the baths, was of great pillars of single stones on every side: the walls also and the floors of the edifices were paved with stones of several colours. He also had cut many and great pits, as reservoirs for water out of rock, at every one of the places that were inhabited . . . and by this contrivance he endeavored to have water for several uses . . . Here was also a road digged from the palace, and leading to the very top of the mountain which yet could not be seen by such as were without the walls."

The Northern Palace, Herod's private villa, was particularly comfortable and luxurious. His private bathhouse contained a *frigidarium* (cold bath), a *tepidarium* (steam bath) and a *caldarium* (a room for hot baths complete with floor heating under black and white tile). In his magnificent dressing room, frescoes resembling marble decorated the walls between sculptured Corinthian columns. On one of the frescoes was the date palm tree, characteristic of the area.

In this setting we can imagine preparations being made for a small banquet with friends of the court. A long, low table has been set for fifteen guests and laden with delicacies. The guests are led into the banquet room where court musicians play softly on lyres and tambours. The meal might begin with a soup similar to Tyche Soup, made with pine nuts, walnuts, and spinach. Tyche was the Roman goddess of fortune to whom Herod erected a large statue at Caesarea, his white marble city on the Mediterranean. (Lost for centuries, this statue was uncovered during the excavation of Caesarea and now stands outside the Sdat Yam Museum.) The banquet would continue with several varieties of meat, such as gazelle, as well as assorted game birds.

It is a remarkable feat to present such exotic fare in this remote spot along the Dead Sea. How could vegetables grow in such an arid land? Answers appeared during Yigael Yadin's excavations. His teams confirmed Josephus's description of torrential rains. During the winter season, after the rains, the desert was covered with flowers and green vegetation. The growing season was lengthened by an ingenious irrigation system using water stored in large cisterns. Such vegetables as legumes, lettuce, artichokes, chicory and melons, along with olive and date trees, were probably grown in Herod's gardens. These foods were preserved, dried, pickled and kept in the vast storerooms located close to the Northern Palace. The remains of grain, pomegranates, walnuts, olives, dates and salt have been discovered on the lower terrace. Herod's taste for Italian wine was confirmed when large jars were discovered, one bearing the inscription "To King Herod of Judea."

TYCHE SOUP
(Spinach and Pine Nut Soup)

1 package (10 ounces) chopped spinach
2 to 3 tablespoons butter
½ cup pine nuts
3 tablespoons chopped walnuts
½ small onion, chopped
2 tablespoons flour
4 cups chicken broth
1½ cups milk
Salt, pepper and nutmeg

Thaw spinach. Melt butter in a heavy saucepan. Add pine nuts and walnuts. Cook, stirring to prevent burning, until nuts turn golden. Add onion and cook for 1 to 2 minutes. Sprinkle flour over all and mix thoroughly. Add chicken broth and spinach. Transfer to deep saucepan and add milk. Bring to boiling point, then season to taste.

Makes 6 to 8 servings.

BRAISED DUCK

1 duck (5 to 6 pounds)
2 onions, chopped
1 clove garlic, minced
2 cups strong chicken broth
Flour for dredging
Salt, pepper and nutmeg to taste
½ pound fresh mushrooms, sliced
2 tablespoons butter

Remove skin and fat from duck; cut into serving pieces. Make marinade by combining the onion, garlic and broth. Soak duck in marinade 2 hours or longer. Drain duck pieces and dredge with flour. Brown in a skillet over high heat. Remove to a casserole and pour on marinade. Cover and simmer 1 hour. Season to taste. Sauté mushrooms lightly in butter and add to the sauce when serving.

Makes 6 to 8 servings.

VALLEY OF ESHCOL ARTICHOKE
(Egg and Artichoke Casserole)

1 package (10 ounces) frozen artichoke hearts, cooked and seasoned
2 tablespoons butter
1 tablespoon lemon juice
6 eggs
Salt and white pepper
4 tablespoons grated Parmesan cheese
Chopped parsley

Place artichokes in a shallow baking dish. Melt butter; add lemon juice and pour over artichokes. Beat eggs until frothy, seasoning to taste. Pour over artichokes. Sprinkle cheese over all. Bake at 375 degrees for 15 minutes, or until eggs are set. Garnish with parsley. Serve at once.

Makes 6 to 8 servings.

ALMOND POACHED PEARS WITH THICKENED CREAM

1½ cups sugar
1 cup water
6 firm ripe pears
½ cup almonds
½ cup confectioners' sugar
Thickened Cream (recipe follows)

Combine sugar and water; bring to a boil. Stir until sugar has dissolved, then reduce heat and simmer gently. Peel pears, leaving them whole with stems on. With a sharp knife or corer, remove seeds from blossom end leaving a cavity. Poach pears gently in the sugar syrup, basting and turning, 8 to 10 minutes or until tender. Do not overcook. Remove pears to a serving dish. Cook syrup until thickened slightly. Grind almonds until fine and combine with confectioners' sugar. Fill each cavity with almond mixture. Pour thickened syrup around pears and chill thoroughly. Serve with Thickened Cream.

THICKENED CREAM

1 cup heavy cream
1 tablespoon sour cream

Combine cream and sour cream; blend thoroughly. Let stand at room temperature until cream has thickened. (The time can vary from 2 to 6 hours according to the weather.) When the cream has thickened, refrigerate for use on desserts and fruits.

Makes 6 servings.

CHAPTER SEVEN

JOHN THE BAPTIST

"In those days came John the Baptist, preaching in the wilderness of Judea" (Matthew 3:1).

Menu

JUDEAN CHICKEN STEW

EZEKIEL BREAD

MIXED FRUITS AND NUTS

CAROB BROWNIES

JOHN THE BAPTIST

When Hebrew boys were six years old they went to synagogue school in their villages during the morning to learn Hebrew customs, Jewish law, Moses' Commandments, and the history of the Patriarchs. If their fathers had a trade, such as carpentry, they would help as apprentices in the afternoon. Mothers in such households had long hours, rising early to grind meal for daily breadmaking, filling and carrying water jars from the village well, making linen and wool tunics from hand-twisted yarn.

The whole family anticipated the annual festival, the Passover, or feast of unleavened bread, celebrated in Jerusalem during the spring, when the city hummed with the flocks of pilgrims coming to commemorate the Israelites' escape from bondage in Egypt.

John the Baptist undoubtedly spent such a childhood. He was a contemporary of Jesus—as a matter of fact, their mothers were cousins. These two who were to influence the world so widely may not have known each other in their youth, but we know of their historic meeting at the Jordan River.

"Now in the fifteenth year of the reign of Tiberius Caesar, Pontius Pilate being governor of Judea, and Herod being tetrarch of Galilee . . . the word of God came unto John the son of Zacharias in the wilderness. And he came into all the country about Jordan, preaching the baptism of repentance for the remission of sins." Thus does Luke (3:1-3) describe the winter of A.D. 28 when John the Baptist began preaching in Jordan and Jesus came to be baptized and to begin his public ministry.

We know that John ignored most creature comforts in his dedication to his mission. The Gospel of St. Mark describes him as "clothed with camel's hair and with a girdle of a skin about his loins; and he did eat locusts and wild honey" (Mark 1:6). We are not exactly certain what is meant by "locusts." Some scholars believe it to be the fruit of the carob tree. The dried or crushed leaves provided good nourishment, and the husks were often fed to the pigs. Carob husks, which he shared with the swine, were the daily fare of the Prodigal Son until he realized the error of his ways and returned home.

Today carob powder is used for a variety of dishes and may be obtained at health food stores. It is an excellent substitute for chocolate. Also available in health food stores are the ingredients for Ezekiel Bread (Ezekiel 4:9): "Take thou also unto thee wheat, and barley, and beans, and lentiles, and millet, and fitches [a kind of wheat according to some scholars, or perhaps dill] and put them in one vessel, and make thee bread thereof . . . three hundred and ninety days shalt thou eat thereof." John's simple tastes could easily have made him aware of that Old Testament recipe given to Ezekiel. Biblical cooks had access to both recipe and ingredients in John's lifetime as they do today. The other dishes given are typical of the simple Judean fare of the period.

JUDEAN CHICKEN STEW

1 stewing chicken (4 to 5 pounds)
2 onions, each studded with 2 cloves
1 lemon, thickly sliced
½ cup chopped celery tops
Pinch of thyme
1 bay leaf
2 cups chicken broth
3 to 4 leeks, sliced in rounds
Salt and pepper
3 tablespoons buttered bread crumbs
Parsley

Wash chicken thoroughly and place in a soup kettle. Add cold water to half cover the bird. Bring to a simmer and cook slowly. Add onions, lemon slices, celery tops, thyme and bay leaf. After 1 hour, add broth and leeks. When chicken is tender, remove to serving dish and carve. Place the slices in a tureen with the soup and vegetables. Season to taste with salt and pepper. When serving, sprinkle with buttered crumbs and parsley.

Makes 6 to 8 servings.

EZEKIEL BREAD

½ cup barley flour
½ cup red lentils
¼ cup soy flour
¼ cup cracked millet
2 teaspoons salt
2 cups boiling water
2 tablespoons olive oil
½ cup warm water
2 packages active dry yeast
½ cup honey
2 cups stone-ground wheat flour
5 to 6 cups all-purpose flour

Whirl lentils in blender until broken into small bits. Combine with soy and barley flours, millet and salt in a large bowl. Pour on boiling water and stir until well-mixed. Add oil and set aside to cool to lukewarm. Pour the warm water over the yeast and let stand until it starts to bubble, about 5 minutes. Combine with cooled grain mixture and add remaining ingredients. Turn out onto a lightly floured board and knead until dough looks smooth and satiny. Place in a greased bowl, cover with a damp towel and let rise until doubled in bulk, about 45 minutes. Punch dough down, turn it around and set aside for 10 minutes. Form into 2 round loaves and place on well greased baking sheets to rise. Let rise 1 hour, then bake at 350 degrees 1 hour or until loaf sounds hollow when thumped on the bottom. Cool on wire racks.

Makes 2 large loaves.

MIXED FRUITS AND NUTS

Select fruits and nuts of contrasting colors and textures and arrange on a flat platter. Figs, plums, dates, pomegranates, grapes, and apricots combined with raisins, pistachio nuts, almonds and walnuts make a very handsome arrangement. A selection of dessert cheeses would be a delicious accompaniment.

CAROB BROWNIES

⅔ cup whole-wheat flour
½ teaspoon baking powder
¼ teaspoon salt
⅓ cup butter
4 tablespoons carob powder
2 eggs
1 cup brown sugar

Combine flour, baking powder and salt. Melt butter and add carob powder. Beat eggs, adding sugar gradually. Add carob-butter mixture and the dry ingredients; mix thoroughly. Spread batter in a well greased 8-inch square pan. Bake at 350 degrees for 25 minutes. Allow brownies to cool in pan, then cut into squares.

Makes 16 (2-inch) brownies.

CHAPTER EIGHT

BETHLEHEM SHEPHERDS

"And there were in the same country shepherds abiding in the field, keeping watch over their flock by night" (Luke 2:8).

Menu

EGGS IN SOUR CREAM
SHEPHERD'S PIE
FRESH GREEN SALAD
GINGERED PRUNES
PINE NUT WAFERS

BETHLEHEM SHEPHERDS

The very nature of sheep, shepherd and flock is woven like golden threads throughout the Bible, the warp and woof of many passages. Herding flocks was an important occupation, affecting all levels of life. The early herders were completely dependent upon the animals for food: "And the people took sheep, and oxen, and calves, and slew them . . . and the people did eat them . . ." (I Samuel 14:32) ; and for income: "And Mesha king of Moab was a sheepmaster and rendered unto the king of Israel an hundred thousand lambs, and an hundred thousand rams, with the wool . . ." (II Kings 3:4) ; for clothing: ". . . should not the shepherds feed the flocks? Ye clothe you with the wool . . . but ye feed not the flock" (Ezekiel 34:2, 3) ; for religious sacrifice: "An altar of earth thou shalt make unto me, and shalt sacrifice thereon thy burnt offerings and thy peace offerings, thy sheep, and thine oxen . . . and I will bless thee" (Exodus 20:24) ; and even for dwelling-places: "And thou shalt make a covering for the tent of rams' skins dyed red . . ." (Exodus 26:14) .

Watching over an immense flock demanded care, attention and skill, for wild animals and robbers were a constant threat. A shepherd and his family ate when they could, simply, but heartily as our menu shows. The children began early to care for sheep; even today very young children can be seen running barefoot over stony hillsides to retrieve a stray lamb and bring it back to the fold.

There was in ancient times and still is today a sheepgate on the north side of the old walled city of Jerusalem, where shepherds still carry on sheep trading. The most popular sheep now, as it has always been, is what is known as the broadtailed sheep, the one with the precious tail that weighs from ten to fifteen pounds. Shepherds' Field still stands outside the gates of modern Bethlehem. Sheep graze over all the hillsides while shepherds still tend them in much the same way as those shepherds who beheld an angel of the Lord and heard his good tidings on that memorable night. These are the fields that Boaz owned, where Ruth gleaned—both in the ancestry of Jesus and David. Their produce, and that of the simple kitchen gardens the shepherds' wives kept, provided the dishes given in this menu.

EGGS IN SOUR CREAM

1¾ cups sour cream
⅓ cup dry bread crumbs
¼ cup melted butter
6 eggs
Salt and white pepper
Grated hard cheese

In a shallow casserole, place 1 cup sour cream; sprinkle with half the crumbs and half the butter. Break eggs and slide them onto sour cream mixture. Cover with remaining sour cream, crumbs and butter. Season to taste. Sprinkle top with grated cheese. Bake at 325 degrees for 20 minutes or until eggs are set.

Makes 6 to 8 servings.

SHEPHERD'S PIE

3½ cups dry bread crumbs
4 tablespoons butter
4 tablespoons chopped parsley
¼ cup bouillon
2 cups finely diced cooked meat (lamb, chicken or beef)
1 cup gravy
1 cup cooked diced carrots
1 cup cooked green peas
1 cup cooked diced turnips
Salt and pepper to taste
Pinch of thyme

Combine crumbs with butter, parsley and bouillon. Toss lightly. Butter a 2-quart charlotte mold or straight-sided casserole. Press crumb mixture firmly on bottom and sides, using half the mixture. Combine meat with gravy and vegetables. Season well and pour into the prepared mold. Press remaining crumbs on top. Bake at 400 degrees for 35 minutes. Let stand 5 minutes before unmolding onto a heated serving platter.

Makes 6 to 8 servings.

NOTES ON GREEN SALAD

Select fresh garden greens, using several varieties of lettuce as well as other greens, such as watercress, fresh mint leaves and fresh herbs. Carefully wash greens and tear into bite-sized pieces, removing all blemishes and tough spines and stems. Wrap greens in towels and place in refrigerator to become crisp. When ready to serve, place them in a glass or ceramic bowl and add desired dressing. Do not use too much dressing (recipe follows). Usually 1/4 cup is sufficient for a large bowl of greens. Add freshly ground salt and pepper to taste and serve at once.

BASIC SALAD DRESSING

3/4 cup olive oil
1/4 cup vinegar
1/4 teaspoon dry mustard
1 teaspoon sugar or honey
Salt and freshly ground pepper

Combine all ingredients and flavor to taste. May be whirled in blender to combine thoroughly.

Makes about 1 cup dressing.

PINE NUT WAFERS

2 egg whites
1½ cups sugar
1½ cups pulverized almonds
½ teaspoon almond extract
½ to ¾ cup pine nuts

Beat egg whites, adding sugar gradually until very stiff. While beating, add pulverized almonds and almond extract. Beat until mixture will hold its shape, adding more almonds if necessary. Grease and flour a baking sheet. Form mixture into small balls and roll in pine nuts. Place on prepared sheet. Flatten each cookie with a dampened spatula. Bake at 425 degrees for 10 to 12 minutes.

Makes about 3 dozen small cookies.

GINGERED PRUNES

18 large prunes
2 whole cloves
½ cup honey
½ cup preserved ginger, chopped, or marmalade
Thickened Cream

Soak prunes in water to cover for 2 hours. Add cloves and honey; simmer until prunes are tender but not mushy. Drain carefully. Remove pits and fill cavities with chopped ginger or marmalade. Place in shallow serving dishes and serve with Thickened Cream.

Makes 6 servings.

CHAPTER NINE

WISE MEN OF THE EAST

". . . behold, there came wise men from the east to Jerusalem . . ." (Matthew 2:1).

Menu

SPICED CIDER

CHALDEAN PRUNES

LEMON CHICKEN

CHICK-PEA SALAD

PERSIAN CREAM RING

GINGER CAKES

WISE MEN OF THE EAST

The "three kings of Orient" are better known through song and fable than from the little told about them in the Bible. We are familiar with stories and pictures showing them presenting their gifts of gold and frankincense and myrrh to the infant Jesus in the manger; but it appears from the Gospel according to St. Matthew (2:1-16) that they appeared in Jerusalem some time after Jesus' birth, were sent by Herod to Bethlehem, and found Jesus there and worshipped him; and, warned by an angel, avoided seeing Herod on the return trip. This aroused his anger and suspicion and led to the slaughter of all male children two years old and under in the Bethlehem region. Even their traditional number, three, and their status as kings—to say nothing of the names of Gaspar, Balthazar and Melchior ascribed to them—are later additions to the story, making the pageantry of Christmas more colorful but not founded on the biblical account.

Yet the Wise Men as we have known them are woven into our observances and holiday memories, in our carols and in our hearts, and should be remembered in this book. And, indeed, whether Kings of Persia, Arabia and Mesopotamia or wandering astronomers, they would have eaten dishes with the oriental touch our menu provides. A further way of recalling the Wise Men is to burn some frankincense or myrrh—obtainable in some health food stores—in your fireplace at Christmas; these dried gums give off an enchanting fragrance when heated.

SPICED CIDER

12 whole cloves
1 teaspoon whole allspice
2 sticks cinnamon
2 quarts apple cider
⅔ cup brown sugar
½ teaspoon ground nutmeg

Tie whole spices in a cheesecloth bag. Heat cider with spices and sugar for 15 to 20 minutes. Serve hot.

Makes 6 to 8 servings.

CHALDEAN PRUNES
(Stuffed Prune Canapés)

4 chicken livers
2 tablespoons butter
16 cooked prunes
Bacon strips

Cut each liver into 4 parts and sauté in butter. Stuff prunes with chicken livers and wrap securely in strips of bacon. Place on rack in a shallow baking pan and bake at 375 degrees until bacon is crisp.

Makes 16 canapés.

LEMON CHICKEN

3 tablespoons whole-wheat flour
Salt and freshly ground pepper
2 2½-pound broiling chickens, cut into serving pieces
4 tablespoons olive oil
Juice and grated rind of 1 lemon
1 cup rich chicken broth
2 tablespoons honey
Lemon slices
Fresh mint sprigs

Combine flour, salt and pepper in a large paper bag. Place a few chicken pieces at a time in the bag and shake vigorously to coat thoroughly with flour mixture. Heat oil in a large skillet and brown coated chicken on all sides. Remove to a shallow baking dish. Sprinkle with lemon juice and grated lemon rind. Pour broth around the chicken. Drizzle honey over all. Cover and bake at 375 degrees for 30 minutes. Uncover and bake 10 to 15 minutes longer. Garnish with thin lemon slices and fresh mint sprigs.

Makes 6 to 8 servings.

CHICK-PEA SALAD

1 cucumber
Salt and pepper to taste
1 can (17 ounces) cooked chick-peas
1 onion, sliced very thin
Salad greens
1 tablespoon chopped fresh mint
2 tablespoons olive oil
1 tablespoon lemon juice

If cucumber has not been treated with preservative, do not peel but slice as thinly as possible. Sprinkle cucumber slices generously with salt and set aside. Rinse chick-peas and drain thoroughly. Rinse and drain cucumber after 15 to 20 minutes. Assemble chick-peas and cucumber slices on a flat serving platter. Sprinkle onion slices over all. Garnish with salad greens and mint. Combine olive oil, lemon juice, salt and pepper; pour over salad.

Makes 6 to 8 servings.

PERSIAN CREAM RING

1 tablespoon gelatin
¼ cup cold milk
2 cups creamed cottage cheese
¾ cup sugar
1 teaspoon vanilla
½ teaspoon grated lemon rind
1 cup cream, whipped

Soak gelatin in milk. Place over hot water to dissolve. Cool to lukewarm, then add to cottage cheese together with the sugar, flavorings and whipped cream. Pour into a 4-cup ring mold and chill in the refrigerator several hours or until set. Unmold onto a serving platter and fill the center with any desired fruit.

Makes 6 to 8 servings.

GINGER CAKES

- **⅔ cup butter**
- **¾ cup light brown sugar, firmly packed**
- **3 tablespoons lukewarm water**
- **2 tablespoons dark molasses**
- **1 teaspoon grated lemon rind**
- **2¼ cups flour**
- **1 teaspoon soda**
- **½ teaspoon salt**
- **1 tablespoon cinnamon**
- **1½ teaspoons ground cloves**
- **1 teaspoon cardamom**
- **½ teaspoon ground ginger**

Cream butter and sugar. Add lukewarm water, molasses and lemon rind, mixing thoroughly. Combine dry ingredients and add slowly, beating very well. Turn out on a lightly floured board and knead until dough is smooth. Chill 1 hour. Roll out on floured surface until very thin. Cut in desired shapes. Bake on a greased cookie sheet at 350 degrees for 6 to 8 minutes. Cool on wire racks.

Makes about 5 dozen small cookies.

CHAPTER TEN

TIBERIUS CAESAR

"Now in the fifteenth year of the reign of Tiberius Caesar . . . the word of God came unto John . . . in the wilderness" (Luke 3:1, 2).

Menu

FISH PÂTÉ WITH SESAME CRISPS
ROAST PHEASANT
WITH
HERB JELLY
KING'S GARDEN ASPARAGUS
ZUCCHINI BOATS
GLAZED ONIONS
ENDIVE AND HAM SALAD
MACAROON PARFAIT

TIBERIUS CAESAR

Augustus's stepson, Tiberius, came to the throne seemingly late in life—at the age of fifty-five—with a reputation for sturdy virtue, bravery and industry. He turned out to be not so near the end of his life as everyone had thought, living and reigning twenty-three more years, nor as virtuous, quickly becoming known for his sloth and self-indulgence. The appointment of Pontius Pilate as Procurator of Judea and the toleration of the excesses of the Herod family as kings of that country are what might be expected from such an emperor.

So was his fondness for the pleasures of the table. It was the era of Apicius, the famous gourmet, cookbook author and inventor of *pâté de foie gras*—an era when the art of good eating and drinking was one of the most absorbing occupations of the rich. At Tiberius's table such delicacies as Avertine calf's liver, pork sausage, mushrooms and elegant soups would be served. The historian Pliny mentions the emperor's fondness for asparagus.

Such exotic foods were not available to the lower classes, who ate simply but substantially and with some variety. Wheat was the staple food, either boiled as porridge or used in a variety of bread recipes. Herbs were used for seasoning.

Breakfast and lunch were simple. At breakfast, bread was dipped in wine or eaten with dates, raisins, honey or olives, and perhaps cheese. Children would have a simple wheat biscuit or bread before school. Lunch was usually served at eleven o'clock—bread or wheat porridge, salad, olives, cheese, fruits, nuts, and possibly leftover cold dishes from yesterday's dinner.

The principal meal of the day was served in late afternoon. Six or seven courses could appear at formal banquets but the customary number was three: the *gustus* (appetizers), the *cena* (main course), and the *secunda mensa* (dessert). The *gustus* consisted of fresh oysters or other shellfish, salted or pickled fresh-water fish, and uncooked vegetables such as lettuce, leeks, and mint. Eggs were almost invariably served. Several courses of fish, meat and fowl were prepared for the *cena* and each guest chose from a variety of dishes—young kid, pheasant or goose, ham, cutlets, or hare. If the *cena* was elaborate, a fish course, probably lamprey, would be served separately. Many delicate sauces accompanied the *cena*, and a wide variety of vegetables. The *secunda mensa* finished the meal, usually a pastry made with honey and chopped nuts and fruit, either fresh or preserved.

Around Rome, enormous gardens supplied abundant artichokes, asparagus, beans, beets, cucumbers, lentils, melons, onions, peas and pumpkins. Nuts and fruits were also plentiful—walnuts, filberts, almonds, peaches, apricots, cherries, pomegranates, apples, pears, plums and quinces. Seasonings such as anise, fennel, mint and mustard were commonly used.

Our menu includes dishes that might have appeared on the Emperor's table or that of a rich or substantial middle-class family. If you wish to share the food of the poor, a standard porridge will do.

FISH PÂTÉ WITH SESAME CRISPS

1 pound fresh salmon
2½ pounds fillet of sole or other white-meat fish
4 egg whites
1¾ cups heavy cream
3 tablespoons chopped fresh dill
2 teaspoons salt
Dash of white pepper
Dash of cayenne pepper
Cucumber slices (garnish)
Serve with Sesame Crisps (recipe follows)

Cut salmon into 2 strips; remove skin and bones and set aside. Cut fillet of sole into 1-inch chunks; put in blender with egg whites, blending a small amount at a time until smooth. Set over a bowl of ice and gradually beat in cream until a fine texture is obtained. Season to taste with dill, salt, white pepper and cayenne. Spoon half the mixture into a buttered terrine or 9×5×3-inch loaf pan. Place salmon slices in the center and cover with remaining sole mixture. Cover carefully with buttered parchment paper. Set terrine in a pan of hot water and bake at 350 degrees for 45 minutes. Chill thoroughly before serving. Garnish with slices of cucumber and lemon.

SESAME CRISPS

2 cups flour
1 teaspoon salt
Dash cayenne pepper
¾ cup butter, broken into walnut-sized pieces
3 tablespoons ice water (about)
1 cup sesame seeds, toasted

Combine flour, salt and cayenne pepper. Mix in butter, using the tips of the fingers to rub the butter and flour mixture together until the texture is like cornmeal. Add ice water and combine lightly. Use more water, if necessary, to make a cohesive dough. Mix in sesame seeds. Chill for half an hour.

Roll dough out very thin, on a lightly floured board. Cut into small shapes as desired and bake on greased cookie sheet at 325 degrees 12 to 15 minutes or until crisp.

Cool and store in airtight containers.

Makes about 10 dozen small crisps.

ROAST PHEASANT WITH HERB JELLY

3 pheasants (2 to 3 pounds each)
¼ cup butter
3 shallots, chopped
2 cups chicken broth
6 strips bacon
2 cups cream
3 tablespoons grated horseradish
Salt and pepper to taste
Herb Jelly (recipe follows)

Split pheasants and brown on all sides in butter. Add shallots and sauté lightly. Add broth and place a bacon strip over each bird. Bake at 375 degrees for 45 minutes, basting often. Remove to a warm serving platter. Cook pan juices over high heat until they are reduced by half. Add cream and horseradish and heat through. Season with salt and pepper. Pour around birds and serve at once with Herb Jelly on the side.

Makes 6 to 8 servings.

HERB JELLY

1 cup fresh herb leaves (rosemary, tarragon or mint)
1½ cups boiling water
5 cups sugar
1 cup cider vinegar
1 bottle (8 ounces) pectin
Green food coloring

Cover leaves with boiling water. Add sugar and vinegar. Stir to dissolve the sugar, then boil for 10 minutes. Strain through a fine sieve or cheesecloth. Add the pectin and a few drops of green coloring. Pour into sterile hot glasses and seal while hot.

Makes about 3 pints.

Tiberius Caesar

KING'S GARDEN ASPARAGUS

5 tablespoons butter
1 cup stale bread crumbs
3 tablespoons finely minced onion
5 eggs
Salt, pepper and nutmeg to taste
1 cup milk
3 cups cooked asparagus
½ cup grated sharp cheese

Grease a deep casserole, using 1 tablespoon butter; sprinkle a few bread crumbs in the bottom. Sauté onion slightly in remaining 4 tablespoons butter. Beat eggs until frothy, then add the onion in butter, remaining bread crumbs, seasonings and milk. Cut asparagus in 1-inch pieces and place in casserole. Pour the mixture over all. Sprinkle with cheese and set casserole in a pan of hot water. Bake at 325 degrees for 35 to 40 minutes or until firm.

Makes 6 to 8 servings.

Random Notes about Herbs

1. Serve a bowl of small, crisp sprigs of watercress as an accompaniment to soups.
2. Add a few mustard or dandelion greens to winter salads.
3. Rub dried herbs in the palm of the hand, using the thumb of the other hand. This releases the aromatic fragrance by the pressure and warmth of the hand.
4. Dry summer herbs by tying in small bunches and hanging in a cool, airy place away from the sun. When dry, strip off the leaves and crumble or, if desired, pulverize them in a mortar. Store in small airtight bottles or jars.

5. Use $\frac{1}{3}$ the amount of dried herbs when substituting them for fresh.
6. Don't keep dried herbs over one year. They lose potency.
7. Try a small amount of chopped tarragon on smoked salmon.
8. Bruise fresh herbs a little to bring out the fragrance.
9. Sow English cress in a shallow dish, lined with damp blotting paper. Place in a sunny window. In 4 to 6 days you will have delicate sprouts with 2 leaves. Snip them off with scissors and use to enhance salads or sandwiches or soups.

ZUCCHINI BOATS

6 small well-shaped zucchini
1 package (10 ounces) frozen green peas
2 tablespoons cream
1 tablespoon butter
Salt and Tabasco sauce
Fresh bread crumbs

Parboil zucchini in boiling salted water for 8 to 10 minutes. Drain and cool slightly. Cook peas according to package directions until tender. Cut zucchini in half lengthwise. With a spoon scoop out seeds and discard, leaving a "boat" for filling. Invert to drain. Place peas in a blender with cream and butter. Whirl until mixture is smooth. Season to taste. Place zucchini boats in a shallow baking dish and fill centers with green pea puree. Sprinkle lightly with fresh bread crumbs. Bake at 375 degrees 15 to 18 minutes or until delicately brown.

Makes 6 to 8 servings.

Tiberius Caesar

GLAZED ONIONS

18 small white onions
3 tablespoons butter
3 tablespoons sugar
¾ cup water (approximate)
1 tablespoon honey
Salt and white pepper to taste

Drop onions into boiling water for a minute to loosen skins. Peel and make a cross in stem end of each onion to prevent it from separating. In a heavy skillet, melt butter and add onions, tossing to brown. Sprinkle with sugar and cook until well coated. Add water to bottom of pan. Reduce heat and simmer until onions are tender, about 25 to 30 minutes. Season with honey, salt and pepper.

Makes 6 servings.

ENDIVE AND HAM SALAD

6 heads endive
1 cup shredded ham
½ cup finely chopped celery
½ cup finely sliced raw string beans
½ cup olive oil
3 tablespoons vinegar
6 tablespoons Roquefort cheese
Salt and pepper to taste
Watercress

Remove center core from endives. Cut them in rounds. Combine with other ingredients and mix lightly. Chill. Serve on bed of watercress.

Makes 6 to 8 servings.

MACAROON PARFAIT

12 Almond Macaroons (recipe follows)
1 cup heavy cream
2 to 3 tablespoons sugar
1 teaspoon vanilla
½ cup undiluted orange juice concentrate
½ cup shredded toasted almonds

Crumble macaroons to make coarse crumbs. Whip cream and flavor with sugar and vanilla. Divide about a third of the crumbs evenly between 6 to 8 parfait glasses; sprinkle with orange juice, add a third of the almonds and a dollop of whipped cream. Repeat, having a swirl of cream on top. Chill for several hours.

Makes 6 to 8 servings.

ALMOND MACAROONS

1 cup almond paste
1 cup plus 2 tablespoons superfine sugar
2 egg whites
½ teaspoon almond extract
Flour

Combine almond paste and sugar; beat thoroughly. Beat in egg whites and almond extract and continue beating until dough is very well combined. Form into small balls, dipping palms of hands in flour to prevent sticking. Place on a lightly oiled cookie sheet. Dampen a clean towel and pat each macaroon to moisten top. Bake at 325 degrees for 15 to 18 minutes or until delicately brown. Remove from sheet carefully while still warm. Cool on wire racks.

Makes about 3 dozen macaroons.

CHAPTER ELEVEN

ARCHELAUS

"But when he [Joseph] heard that Archelaus did reign in Judea . . . he came and dwelt in a city called Nazareth . . ." (Matthew 2:22, 23).

Menu

SHRIMP ROULADE

ORANGE GAME HENS

WITH

PUNGENT FRUIT SAUCE

BAKED ZUCCHINI

MOLDED WATERCRESS SALAD

ALMOND TORTE

WITH

PEACH SAUCE

ARCHELAUS

Though not the monster his father, Herod the Great, had been, Archelaus managed to achieve the distinction of being one of the most disliked of his family. After a family controversy and a popular uprising following his father's death, the Romans stepped in and gave Archelaus control of part of Palestine, Idumaea, Judea and Samaria, which he ruled both brutally and ineptly.

He taxed the people heavily in order to rebuild the splendid palace at Jericho. No doubt the food he served was rare and lavish. The extensive network of Roman shipping lanes enabled him to import delicacies from all parts of the empire, even cherries from as far away as Asia Minor. Seafood and shellfish were readily available as Caesarea, the principal port of Samaria, supported a large fishing fleet.

For a decade Archelaus vainly tried to impose his authority on Judea. In A.D. 6 he again went to Rome to placate Augustus, but the Emperor would no longer tolerate his excesses. He deposed Archelaus and banished him to Vienne in southern Gaul. Judea became a Roman province.

Our menu is intended to give a taste of the food of the time and place, not to fix this deplorable ruler in memory. It would be uncharitable, but understandable, to hope he missed such dishes as these in his exile.

SHRIMP ROULADE

6 tablespoons butter
½ cup flour
2 cups milk
5 eggs, separated
1 teaspoon sugar
Salt and pepper to taste
Shrimp Filling (recipe follows)

In a heavy saucepan, melt butter. Add flour and cook until bubbling and golden. Gradually add milk and cook, stirring constantly, until sauce is thickened. Add egg yolks, one at a time, beating well after each addition. Season to taste. Beat egg whites with sugar until stiff; fold into yolk mixture. Prepare an 11 × 15-inch jelly roll pan. Butter generously, line with wax paper and butter again. Spread batter smoothly in pan and bake at 325 degrees 30 to 40 minutes or until delicately brown and firm to the touch. Turn out on a clean towel; remove the wax paper and roll up in the towel. Allow to rest in the towel 10 minutes. Unroll and fill with Shrimp Filling. Roll up once more and place in shallow baking dish. Heat at 350 degrees 10 to 12 minutes.

SHRIMP FILLING

1 package (3 ounces) cream cheese
1 pint sour cream
2 cups chopped cooked shrimp
Salt and pepper to taste

Soften cream cheese with the sour cream. Combine with remaining ingredients. Use part of mixture as filling for the roulade. Pass remaining portion separately as a sauce.

Note: Creamed mushrooms make a delicious filling for the roulade. Other creamed foods may be substituted.

Makes 6 to 8 servings.

ORANGE GAME HENS WITH PUNGENT FRUIT SAUCE

3 Rock Cornish game hens (1¼ pounds each) thawed, split and halved
1 tablespoon grated ginger root *or* **1½ teaspoons ground ginger**
3 tablespoons honey
Salt
Orange slices (garnish)
Pungent Fruit Sauce (recipe follows)

Wipe hens dry with paper towels. Place on rack in broiler pan. Combine ginger and honey; brush skin surface of hens with mixture. Broil, skin side up, until brown and shining. Reduce oven temperature to 350 degrees and bake 25 to 30 minutes longer or until hens are tender. Baste several times with pan drippings. Sprinkle with salt. Serve hot or cold, garnished with orange slices. Accompany with Pungent Fruit Sauce.

Note: Squab or small broilers may be used.

Makes 6 servings.

PUNGENT FRUIT SAUCE

½ cup orange marmalade
2 tablespoons lemon juice
2 tablespoons orange juice
2 teaspoons grated horseradish
¼ teaspoon ground ginger
½ teaspoon hot mustard

Place all the ingredients in a blender and whirl for 2 minutes. Allow to stand 30 minutes before using.

Makes 1 cup sauce.

BAKED ZUCCHINI

6 small zucchini
2 to 3 tablespoons oil or butter
1 onion, thinly sliced
Salt and pepper to taste
½ cup grated Parmesan cheese

Wash zucchini thoroughly and grate or slice finely. Heat oil or butter in a heavy casserole. Toss onion rings in the oil; add zucchini and mix slightly. Season with salt and pepper. Sprinkle with grated cheese and bake at 375 degrees for 15 to 20 minutes.

Makes 6 to 8 servings.

MOLDED WATERCRESS SALAD

2 bunches watercress
2 cups rich chicken broth
1½ tablespoons gelatin
Salt and Tabasco sauce to taste
Juice and grated rind of 1 lemon
Salad greens (garnish)

Remove tough stems from watercress. Place the leaves in a blender with 1 cup broth and blend thoroughly. Soak gelatin in ¼ cup cold broth, then dissolve in ¾ cup hot broth. Combine liquids and season with salt, Tabasco sauce, lemon juice and rind. Place in a 4-cup ring mold and chill several hours or until set. Unmold onto a chilled serving platter and garnish with crisp salad greens. Fill center with celery root remoulade, cottage cheese or any other desired filling.

Makes 6 to 8 servings.

ALMOND TORTE WITH PEACH SAUCE

1¾ cups unblanched almonds
½ cup crushed arrowroot biscuits
1 teaspoon baking powder
½ cup soft butter
1¼ cups sugar
6 eggs, separated
1 teaspoon vanilla
1½ cups sweetened whipped cream flavored with almond extract
½ cup shredded toasted almonds
Peach Sauce (recipe follows)

Whirl unblanched almonds in a blender until pulverized. Combine with arrowroot crumbs and baking powder. Cream butter thoroughly, adding ¾ cup sugar gradually, and beating until the mixture is light and lemon colored. Add egg yolks, one at a time, beating well after each addition. Beat egg whites until fluffy and add the remaining ½ cup of sugar by spoonfuls, beating well after each addition. Combine egg yolk mixture and whites, folding in the dry ingredients very carefully at the same time. Add the vanilla.

Grease and flour an 8-or-9-inch spring-form pan. Bake the torte at 325 degrees for 1 hour or until top is springy when gently pressed. When cool, cut the torte in two or three layers. Fill and ice with sweetened whipped cream to which a few drops of almond flavoring have been added. Press the toasted almonds around the sides of the cake.

Makes an 8- or 9-inch cake.

PEACH SAUCE

1 cup mashed fresh or frozen peaches
1 teaspoon cornstarch (arrowroot may be used)
1 tablespoon lemon juice
Sugar to taste

Combine peaches with cornstarch and heat gently until mixture thickens. Add lemon juice and sugar, if needed. This sauce may be served over ice cream, plain cakes or poached pears.

Makes 1 cup sauce.

CHAPTER TWELVE

DISCIPLES ON THE GALILEAN SHORE

"And Jesus, walking by the sea of Galilee, saw two brethren, Simon called Peter, and Andrew his brother, casting a net into the sea: for they were fishers. And he saith unto them, Follow me, and I will make you fishers of men. . . . And they straightway left their nets and followed him" (Matthew 4:18-20).

Menu

CUCUMBER BISQUE

CHARCOAL BROILED FISH

WITH

HONEYCOMB

BARLEY LOAVES

ALMOND CHEESE SPREAD

CAPERNAUM FRUITS

DISCIPLES ON THE GALILEAN SHORE

Fishing was the primary occupation all along the shores of the Sea of Galilee. During the day fishermen mended their nets, repaired their boats, gossiped and prepared for the nighttime fishing expeditions. Women and children cleaned, salted and preserved fish for shipping northward to Damascus, south to Jerusalem and across the Mediterranean to Spain.

Along the north shore of the Sea of Galilee lies the fertile plain of Gennesaret where Jesus walked and taught. The historian Josephus describes it as "a stretch of country wonderful in its characteristics and in its beauty. Thanks to the rich soil, there is not a plant that does not flourish there, and the inhabitants grow everything; the air is so temperate that it suits the most diverse species. . . . Walnuts, the most winter-loving of trees, flourish in abundance, as do palm, which thrive on heat, side by side with the figs and olives for which a milder air is indicated. One might deem it nature's crowning achievement to force together into one spot natural enemies and to bring the seasons into healthy rivalry, each as it were laying claim to the region. For not only does it produce the most surprisingly diverse fruits; it maintains a continuous supply. Those royal fruits, the grape and the fig, it furnishes for ten months on end, the most ripening on the trees all year round; for apart from the temperate atmosphere it is watered by a spring with great fertilizing power known locally as Capharnaum" (Flavius Josephus, *The Jewish War,* Book 3, Chapter VI, 8).

According to Luke, this was the site of the feeding of the multitude. The large crowd had listened all day to Jesus preaching. When afternoon became evening, Jesus asked where bread might be bought for so many. A disciple found a lad with five barley loaves and two fishes. Jesus took the loaves and fishes and "blessed them and brake . . . And they did eat and were all filled: and there was taken up of fragments that remained to them twelve baskets" (Luke 9:16, 17).

It was also on the shores of the Sea of Galilee that Jesus appeared to his disciples after his crucifixion. The disciples, thoroughly dejected, had returned to their fishing jobs. As they were rowing to shore one morning with empty nets after a night of fishing, they saw a man standing on the shore. "Jesus stood on the shore. But the disciples knew not that it was Jesus. Then Jesus saith unto them, Children have ye any meat? They answered him, No. And he said unto them, Cast the net on the right side of the ship and ye shall find. They cast therefore, and now they were not able to draw it for the multitude of fishes" (John 21:4-6). Luke tells of the appearance of Jesus behind locked doors in their midst while they were speaking about him. "And while they believed not for joy . . . he said unto them, Have ye here any meat? And they gave him a piece of broiled fish, and of an honeycomb" (Luke 24:41, 42).

After eating with them he explained parts of the Scriptures as they applied to himself, beginning with Moses and the prophets. They understood, and as he walked with them to Bethany he disappeared from their sight—but not from their hearts—for they returned to Jerusalem with joy, inspired to fulfill their missions.

CUCUMBER BISQUE

3 small cucumbers
2 teaspoons salt
2 cups yogurt
2 ice cubes
½ cup light cream
1 teaspoon chopped fresh dill
2 teaspoons chopped parsley
Salt and white pepper to taste

Peel and dice cucumbers, discarding the seeds. Sprinkle with 2 teaspoons salt and let stand 30 minutes. Rinse in cold water and drain thoroughly. Place in a blender with yogurt and ice cubes; cover and whirl until smooth. Combine with remaining ingredients. Serve chilled.

Makes 6 to 8 servings.

CHARCOAL BROILED FISH WITH HONEYCOMB

6 to 8 thin fish fillets (flounder, sole or haddock)
2 tablespoons butter
Salt and pepper to taste
1 lemon, thinly sliced
2 tablespoons chopped parsley
½ pound honey in the comb

Blot the fish fillets dry with paper towels. Melt 1 tablespoon butter in a shallow baking dish, then arrange fillets in single layer and top with remaining 1 tablespoon butter. Season with salt and pepper. Broil quickly, but do not overcook. Fish is done when the flesh is opaque and flakes easily when pricked with a fork. Serve garnished with lemon slices and chopped parsley. Serve the honeycomb in a separate dish as an unusual accompaniment.

Note: This is an approximation of the only meal that Jesus ate which is recorded in the Bible. (Luke 24:42-43).

Makes 6 servings.

BARLEY LOAVES

2 cups barley flour
1½ to 2 cups unbleached flour
2 packages active dry yeast
3 tablespoons lukewarm water
1¼ cups chicken broth
2 tablespoons honey
1 teaspoon salt
3 tablespoons oil

Combine flours in a large bowl. Dissolve yeast in lukewarm water. Add to flours with remaining ingredients and mix thoroughly. Turn out on a floured surface and knead until dough is elastic and smooth. Cover with a damp towel and allow to rise 30 to 40 minutes. Punch down and knead again. Form into two loaves and allow to rise in well-greased 9×5×3-inch loaf pans until well rounded (about 30 minutes). Bake at 375 degrees for about 45 minutes or until done.

Makes 2 loaves.

ALMOND CHEESE SPREAD

2 teaspoons butter
⅓ cup shredded almonds
1 tablespoon finely chopped dill pickle
1 tablespoon chutney
2 teaspoons grated horseradish
1 package (3 ounces) cream cheese
1 teaspoon prepared mustard
Dash of cayenne pepper
Salt to taste
Cream (optional)
Fried toast rounds (recipe follows)
1 teaspoon chopped chives
Minced parsley

Melt butter in a skillet and add almonds. Cook, stirring constantly to prevent scorching, until delicately brown. Add pickle, chutney, horseradish, salt, mustard and cayenne; then mix thoroughly. Soften cream cheese, adding a few drops of cream if needed, to make a smooth mixture. Spread cream cheese on toast rounds. Cover with some of the almond mixture and garnish with a mixture of chives and parsley.

Note: To make fried toast rounds, cut fresh bread with a biscuit cutter in the size and shape desired. In a heavy skillet, melt a small amount of butter and fry the bread pieces until they are delicately brown on each side.

Makes about 1 cup of spread.

CAPERNAUM FRUITS
(Baked Mixed Fruits)

1 can (30 ounces) cling peaches
1 can (30 ounces) pear halves
1 can (30 ounces) pineapple slices
¾ cup light brown sugar, firmly packed
Juice of 1 lime
2 to 3 tablespoons butter

Drain fruits thoroughly. Use juices for other purposes. In saucepan, combine sugar, lime juice and butter; heat until butter is melted. Place fruits in shallow baking dish and pour the sauce over all. Bake, uncovered, at 325 degrees 1 hour.

Note: Any desired combinations of fruits may be used. Fresh fruits are delicious when prepared this way.

Makes 6 to 8 servings.

CHAPTER THIRTEEN

ANTIPAS

". . . Herod on his birthday made a supper to his lords, high captains, and chief estates of Galilee" (Mark 6:21).

Menu

POMEGRANATE SOUP

HERODIAN VEAL

SPINACH CUSTARD PIE

ROYAL BEET SALAD

WALNUT TORTE

ANTIPAS

Antipas, son of Herod the Great, fared politically better than his inept and unpopular brother Archelaus. As ruler of Galilee he enjoyed the favor of Augustus and later cultivated the good will of Tiberius, for whom he named his new capital on the Dead Sea. Antipas's cunning was well known; Jesus referred to him as "the fox."

Antipas, whom the Gospels call simply Herod, lived extravagantly and ate sumptuously, often entertaining the Emperor himself. Banqueting was a favorite pastime that gave his cooks every opportunity to surpass previous triumphs. You will notice that on our menu is a Royal Beet Salad. According to Pliny two kinds of beets were grown, a summer and winter variety.

Antipas's downfall began with the "birthday supper" mentioned in Mark 6:21, for it was then that his niece and stepdaughter Salome danced so well that she was granted whatever she might ask. What she wanted turned out to be the head of John the Baptist—her mother Herodias, once married to Antipas's half-brother, was enraged at John's blunt comments on the morality of her remarriage. The storm aroused by John's murder fatally weakened Antipas's authority. It was to Antipas, who was in Jerusalem for Passover, that Pontius Pilate sent Jesus during his trial, on the pretext that Jesus was a Galilean. In A.D. 39, Antipas, was accused by his nephew of planning a revolt against the Romans; as he was unable to explain satisfactorily what he meant to do with the large number of arms he had gathered, the Emperor banished him to Gaul.

POMEGRANATE SOUP

½ pound ground lean beef
1 small onion, finely chopped
½ cup chopped scallions
2 tablespoons sugar
2 teaspoons salt (or to taste)
½ cup raw rice
8 cups water
1 cup chopped parsley
1 tablespoon chopped mint
1 tablespoon lime juice
1 cup pomegranate juice (orange juice concentrate may be substituted)

Combine ground meat, onion, scallions, sugar and salt. Form into small balls. Boil rice in the water for 15 minutes. Add meatballs, parsley, mint and juices. Simmer 5 to 7 minutes. Correct seasonings. Serve hot or cold.

Makes 6 to 8 servings.

HERODIAN VEAL

2½ pounds veal, thinly sliced (scaloppine)
4 tablespoons olive oil
Juice of 3 lemons
Salt and pepper to taste
Chopped parsley (garnish)
Lemon slices (garnish)

Pound veal slices between pieces of wax paper. In a heavy skillet, heat oil and quickly sear veal on both sides.

Remove to a warm serving dish. Deglaze skillet with the lemon juice. Season veal with salt and pepper. Pour on hot lemon juice. Garnish with chopped parsley and thin slices of lemon.

Makes 6 to 8 servings.

SPINACH CUSTARD PIE

1½ cups light cream
4 eggs, lightly beaten
½ small onion, chopped fine
2 tablespoons butter
4 cups finely chopped spinach
Salt, pepper and nutmeg to taste
½ cup grated Gruyère cheese
Unbaked 9-inch pie shell
¼ cup grated Parmesan cheese

Heat the cream, then cool slightly; gradually beat in eggs. Sauté onion in butter until limp. Add spinach, seasonings and Gruyère cheese. Add egg mixture and combine thoroughly. Pour into pie shell. Sprinkle with Parmesan cheese. Bake at 375 degrees for 30 minutes or until firm.

Note: All pies are improved if the empty shell is baked at 400 degrees for 10 minutes, cooled and then filled.

Makes a 9-inch pie.

ROYAL BEET SALAD

4 whole cooked beets
1 or 2 scallions, minced
Chicory
2 tablespoons olive oil
Juice of ½ lemon
1 teaspoon vinegar
Salt and freshly ground pepper to taste

Slice beets thinly into a glass bowl. Sprinkle with scallions. Tear chicory into bite-sized pieces, discarding tough or wilted parts. Combine oil, lemon juice, vinegar, salt and pepper; mix thoroughly. Pour over salad and toss lightly.

Makes 6 to 8 servings.

WALNUT TORTE

5 eggs, separated
1 teaspoon vanilla
1½ cups confectioners' sugar
1 cup flour
½ teaspoon baking powder
Dash of salt
1 cup coarsely chopped walnuts
1½ cups heavy cream, whipped

Beat egg yolks with vanilla, adding sugar gradually, until mixture is thick and lemon colored. Sift flour and baking powder over yolks. Add walnuts. Beat egg whites with salt until stiff and glossy but not too firm; fold into yolk mixture. Divide mixture evenly in 2 lightly-buttered 8-inch layer cake pans. Bake at 325 degrees 25 to 30 minutes or until firm to the touch. Cool layers on wire racks then frost with sweetened whipped cream.

Makes an 8-inch cake.

CHAPTER FOURTEEN

MARY AND MARTHA

"There they made . . . a supper; and Martha served . . ." (John 12:2).

Menu

BETHANY OMELET
WITH
VEGETABLES
POT ROAST
WITH
SOUR CREAM
UPSIDE-DOWN APPLE CAKE

MARY AND MARTHA

"Now it came to pass, as they went, that he [Jesus] entered into a certain village: and a certain woman named Martha received him into her house. And she had a sister called Mary . . ." (Luke 10:38-39).

These two women and their brother Lazarus were like his own family to Jesus. According to the Gospel of John they lived in Bethany near Jerusalem. Both Gospels, Luke and John, present Martha as a woman who enjoys entertaining friends in her home. Mary, more interested in their honored guest's teaching than in domestic chores, "sat at Jesus' feet, and heard his word" (Luke 10:39).

With Martha's flair for entertaining, their home must have been attractive and comfortable. It is easy to picture the flurry of kitchen activity preparing favorite recipes; omelet with fresh vegetables from the garden, a well-seasoned pot roast, a light pita, and a sweet apple cake cooked right in the pan. Jesus, sensing Martha's impatience with Mary for not helping with dinner ". . . said unto her, Martha, Martha, thou art careful and troubled about many things: But one thing is needful: and Mary hath chosen that good part . . ." (Luke 10:41, 42).

BETHANY OMELET WITH VEGETABLES

1½ tablespoons butter
1 tablespoon minced onion
½ cup chopped lamb
¼ pound mushrooms, chopped
6 eggs
½ cup cream
Salt and freshly ground pepper to taste
2 tablespoons grated hard cheese

Melt butter in a heavy skillet. Sauté onion, then add lamb and mushrooms and toss in butter to heat. Combine eggs with cream and seasonings; pour over mixture in skillet. Heat slowly, then add cheese and glaze in the oven. Serve at once.

Makes 6 to 8 servings.

POT ROAST WITH SOUR CREAM

¼ cup olive oil
1 eye-of-the-round pot roast (5 to 6 pounds)
2 medium onions, chopped
1 clove garlic (optional)
2 tablespoons flour
1 quart water
2 bay leaves
Salt and pepper to taste
¼ teaspoon Herbs of Kidron
¼ teaspoon ground ginger
1 pint sour cream

In a deep heavy casserole, brown roast on all sides in olive oil. Remove and set aside. In the same pan, sauté onion with garlic until limp. Sprinkle on flour and cook a moment. Return meat to pan; add water and seasonings. Cover tightly and either simmer or bake at 325 degrees for 2 hours or until almost tender. Add sour cream and continue cooking until roast is tender. Remove fat from top of gravy. Correct seasonings and serve in thin slices. Accompany with Pita Bread.

Makes 8 to 10 servings.

UPSIDE-DOWN APPLE CAKE

¼ cup butter
2 cups sliced apples
½ cup chopped almonds
1 egg
½ cup sugar
1½ cups flour
2 teaspoons baking powder
½ teaspoon salt
Grated rind of 1 orange
½ cup milk

In a 9-inch skillet, melt butter. Add apples and nuts. Set aside. Beat egg, adding sugar gradually. Combine dry ingredients, egg mixture and orange rind; add milk and mix thoroughly. Pour batter over apples in skillet. Bake at 325 degrees 35 minutes or until cake is firm. Loosen edges and invert cake on serving plate. Serve with thick cream, if desired.

Note: Apricots, peaches or plums may be substituted for the apples.

Makes a 9-inch cake.

CHAPTER FIFTEEN

YOUNG SAUL OF TARSUS

"I am a man which am a Jew of Tarsus, a city in Cilicia . . ." (Acts 21:39).

Menu

SKEWERED LAMB OF CILICIA

STUFFED CUCUMBERS

ANATOLIAN VEGETABLES

HONEY OATMEAL CAKE

WITH

DAMASCUS SAUCE

YOUNG SAUL OF TARSUS

Saul was born during the reign of Caesar Augustus into a Jewish family of Tarsus, capital of Cilicia, in Asia Minor (modern Turkey). His father was a Roman citizen and the boy was later to be known by his Roman name, Paul. He was brought up in the traditional Jewish manner, learning Hebrew customs, Jewish law, Moses' Commandments and the history of the Patriarchs. He also learned a trade, tent making. Then to further his education, his father sent him to Jerusalem to study under the great rabbi Gamaliel. Becoming a Pharisee zealot, Saul and a band of followers undertook to search out and persecute the followers of Christ, who they felt would prove dangerous to the Jews. Saul himself was involved with the stoning of St. Stephen (Acts 7:60, 8:1).

After the remarkable conversion on the road to Damascus that blinded and enlightened him simultaneously, the Tarsian, baptized in the new faith, returned home to preach Christianity under his new name, Paul. "For ye are all the children of God by faith in Christ Jesus . . . There is neither Jew nor Greek" (Galatians 3:26, 28).

Tarsus was a thriving cosmopolitan city, famous for its schools and lively politics. The city had access to the Mediterranean as well as to a gap in the Taurus Mountains used by camel caravans from the heart of Asia Minor. We have tried to reflect this blending of oriental and western cultures in our menu. The large and fertile Plain of Cilicia produced many vegetables, and grains. Skewered lamb has been a favorite dish in this area for centuries, seasoned as it is with the local herbs and spices. Brass skewers are still made and used throughout Turkey today.

SKEWERED LAMB OF CILICIA
(Lamb Kebobs)

3 pounds leg of lamb, cut in cubes
1 medium onion, chopped
1 garlic clove, minced
½ teaspoon salt
½ teaspoon pepper
½ teaspoon ground ginger
½ teaspoon cumin
9 whole cloves
1 bay leaf
½ teaspoon rosemary
½ teaspoon Herbs of Kidron
¼ cup olive oil
⅓ cup honey
2 tablespoons vinegar
1 teaspoon dried mint flakes
Juice and grated rind of 1 lemon

Trim lamb cubes, removing all fat. Mix together remaining ingredients. Allow lamb to marinate in this mixture for several hours. Drain and string chunks of lamb on skewers. Place skewers on rack in broiling pan and broil under very hot heat or cook over charcoal until done to taste (about 10 to 12 minutes on each side).

Makes 6 to 8 servings.

STUFFED CUCUMBERS

1 cup date juice*
6 small cucumbers
3 tablespoons butter
3 tablespoons minced onion
3 cups cooked rice
2 tablespoons chopped pimiento
Salt and pepper
1 cup grated sharp cheese

*To prepare date juice, cover ½ pound dried dates with boiling water. Simmer gently 30 to 40 minutes. Strain and use as directed.

If cucumbers are young and tender, do not peel; otherwise, peel. Slice in half lengthwise. With a sharp spoon, scoop out and discard seeds. Place cucumber boats in a shallow pan. In a large skillet, melt butter and sauté onion until transparent. Add rice and toss to coat thoroughly. Add pimiento and mix. Season to taste. Lightly fill cucumber boats with rice mixture. Spoon approximately 1 tablespoon date juice on each. Sprinkle with cheese. Bake at 375 degrees 15 to 18 minutes or until heated through.

Note: Leftover meat, diced or ground, or any combination of vegetables may be added to the rice.

Makes 6 servings.

ANATOLIAN VEGETABLES

½ cup butter or margarine
½ cup dry bread crumbs
4 slices bread, crusts removed
½ cup cream
¾ cup cooked, chopped and drained spinach
½ cup finely chopped asparagus or string beans
¼ cup chopped mushrooms
1 tablespoon grated onion
Salt and pepper to taste
5 eggs, separated
2 to 3 tablespoons grated Parmesan cheese
2 tablespoons chopped parsley

Prepare a 1-quart charlotte mold or straight-sided casserole. Butter generously and dust with bread crumbs. Soak bread slices in cream, then squeeze out excess moisture. Combine with vegetables, seasonings and egg yolks. Beat egg whites until stiff but not dry and fold into the mixture. Place in prepared pan and cover with foil. Set the pan in another pan of water and bake at 375 degrees for 40 to 50 minutes or until firm. Remove foil and allow top to become delicately brown. Loosen edges with spatula and turn out on to a warm serving platter. Dust with Parmesan cheese and parsley.

Makes 6 to 8 servings.

Young Saul

HONEY OATMEAL CAKE WITH DAMASCUS SAUCE

1½ cups water
1 cup instant oatmeal
½ cup butter
1 cup sugar
1 cup brown sugar
3 eggs
3 tablespoons dark corn syrup
1½ cups flour
1 teaspoon each soda, cinnamon and salt
¼ teaspoon freshly ground nutmeg
Damascus Sauce (recipe follows)

Bring water to a boil and add oatmeal. Cook briefly until mixture thickens. Allow to cool slightly. Cream butter and sugars. Add eggs, one at a time, beating well after each addition. Mix in corn syrup, cooled oatmeal and then the dry ingredients. Pour batter into a greased 9-inch tube pan. Bake at 350 degrees 50 minutes or until a straw inserted in cake comes out clean.

Makes a 9-inch cake.

DAMASCUS SAUCE

2 tablespoons butter
¾ cup dark brown sugar
3 tablespoons cream
1 cup chopped walnuts

Heat butter and sugar with the cream until butter melts and sugar dissolves. Add nuts and spread on warm cake. Glaze under broiler until delicately brown.

Makes about 1¾ cups sauce.

CHAPTER SIXTEEN

LYDIA, SELLER OF PURPLE

"And a certain woman named Lydia, a seller of purple. . . . besought us, saying, If ye have judged me to be faithful to the Lord, come into my house, and abide there" (Acts 16: 14, 15).

Menu

CHILLED SQUASH SOUP

CRAB AEGEAN

HONEYED PARSNIPS

COUNTRY SALAD

MACEDONIAN TEA LOAF

WITH

ALMOND SAUCE

LYDIA, SELLER OF PURPLE

It was in Antioch, then the largest city in the Mediterranean world after Rome and Alexandria, that Paul's apostolic mission really began: "And the disciples were called Christians first in Antioch" (Acts 11:26). Preaching, teaching, writing and healing, Paul traveled more than 12,000 miles in four great journeys. He traversed Asia Minor, crossed the Aegean Sea to Greece, and sailed through the Mediterranean to Crete, Malta, and Rome.

On the second of these missionary journeys Paul, together with Silas, Luke and Timothy, crossed into Europe from Troas, near Homer's Troy. Sailing across the Aegean to Neapolis, the modern Kavalla in Macedonia, he proceeded inland to nearby Philippi. It was outside the walls of Philippi that Paul and his missionaries baptized a well-to-do woman named Lydia, together with her household. These were probably Paul's first Christian converts in Europe. "And on the sabbath we went out of the city by a river side, where prayer was wont to be made ... and spake unto the women who had resorted thither. And a certain woman named Lydia, a seller of purple, of the city of Thyatira, which worshipped God, heard us: whose heart the Lord opened, that she attended unto the things which were spoken of Paul" (Acts 16:13, 14).

Philippi was a Roman colony and in its marketplace could be found goods and foodstuffs from many other Roman colonies. A shopping list for a substantial household like Lydia's must have included spices from India; oysters, cheese, honey and carpets from Asia Minor; and glass, linen and alabaster from Egypt. Her kitchen servants might have bought fresh Aegean crabs from a local fisherman as well as bunches of tender parsnips and an assortment of fresh vegetables for a country salad.

Fresh food was abundant all through the marketplace, for Philippi was located in a fertile plain where olive trees, fruits and vegetables flourished. Fish was plentiful too, for the Greeks of Neapolis could fish in the waters of both the Aegean and Mediterranean seas.

CHILLED SQUASH SOUP

1 tablespoon butter
3 small onions, finely minced
1 medium yellow squash
1 quart rich chicken broth
1 pint light cream
Salt, pepper and nutmeg to taste
Lemon slices

In a heavy skillet, melt butter and sauté onions until limp. Do not brown. Cut unpeeled squash into small dice and simmer in broth until tender, about 15 minutes. Add onion. Whirl mixture in a blender until smooth. Strain and add cream. Season to taste. Chill before serving. Garnish with thin lemon slices.

Makes 6 to 8 servings.

CRAB AEGEAN
(Crabmeat au Gratin)

1 tablespoon minced shallots
2 tablespoons butter
2 tablespoons lemon juice
1 tablespoon flour
2 egg yolks, lightly beaten
½ cup light cream
1 pound fresh lump crabmeat
Salt, pepper and Tabasco sauce to taste
Grated Parmesan cheese
Bread crumbs

Sauté shallots in butter until limp. Add lemon juice and cook until reduced to about 1 tablespoon. Sprinkle flour over and cook for a moment. Combine egg yolks and cream. Pour over shallot mixture and cook over low heat, stirring constantly, until thickened. Pick over crabmeat carefully. Combine with sauce being careful not to break up crabmeat. Season to taste. Pile lightly in a shallow casserole or individual shells. Sprinkle with grated cheese and crumbs. Bake at 450 degrees for 10 minutes or until delicately browned on top.

Makes 4 servings.

HONEYED PARSNIPS

3 cups diced parsnips
1 bay leaf
3 tablespoons honey
3 tablespoons butter or margarine
Salt and pepper to taste
Pinch of cumin

Cook parsnips in rapidly boiling water with the bay leaf until tender, about 6 to 8 minutes. Drain thoroughly and add remaining ingredients. Place in a blender and whirl until smooth or mash with a fork. When ready to serve, reheat over gentle heat.

Makes 6 to 8 servings.

COUNTRY SALAD
(Nicoise)

2 cups diced cooked potatoes
2 cups cooked green beans
½ cup Basic Salad Dressing
Salt and freshly ground pepper
1 clove garlic
3 hard-cooked eggs, quartered
¾ cup tuna fish chunks
Pitted ripe olives
12 anchovy fillets

Toss potatoes and beans in salad dressing to coat thoroughly. Season with salt and freshly ground pepper. Cut garlic clove in half and rub the inside of a salad bowl. Arrange potatoes and beans in the bowl and surround with egg quarters. Place tuna chunks in the center and decorate with olives and anchovy fillets.

Makes 6 servings.

MACEDONIAN TEA LOAF WITH ALMOND SAUCE

¼ cup honey
⅔ cup brown sugar
1 teaspoon salt
3 tablespoons butter or margarine
½ cup chopped dates
½ cup chopped dried apricots
1 cup milk
1 egg
2 teaspoons lemon juice
4 teaspoons baking powder

¼ teaspoon soda
2½ cups flour
⅓ cup bran
Almond Sauce (recipe follows)

Combine honey, sugar, salt, butter or margarine, fruits and milk in a saucepan. Heat until butter melts. Set aside to cool. Grease 9×5×3-inch loaf pans; line bottoms with brown paper and grease again. Add egg and lemon juice to liquids, then add dry ingredients. Mix thoroughly but do not beat. Fill pans ⅔ full. Bake at 350 degrees 1 hour. Cool on wire racks. Serve with Almond Sauce.

Makes 2 loaf cakes.

ALMOND SAUCE

1 cup blanched almonds
2 teaspoons grated orange peel
¼ teaspoon almond extract
2 egg yolks
½ cup superfine sugar
1 cup heavy cream

Grind almonds until very fine in a blender or nut grinder. Place them in a mortar with orange peel and pound thoroughly. Transfer to a saucepan and add almond extract, sugar and egg yolks. Add cream gradually, stirring constantly. Cook over low heat, stirring, until sauce is slightly thickened and foamy. Do not boil.

Makes about 1½ cups sauce.

CHAPTER SEVENTEEN

PAUL IN GREECE

". . . Paul called unto him the disciples and embraced them, and departed for to go into Macedonia. And when he had gone over those parts, and had given them much exhortation, he came into Greece" (Acts 20:1, 2).

Menu

JERUSALEM ALMOND CHICKEN

PITA POCKETS

CREAMED TURNIPS

ISTHMUS WREATH CAKE

PAUL IN GREECE

One of Paul's key destinations for his missionary work was Athens, still the intellectual capital of the world. The sophisticated Greeks did not give Paul much of a hearing. "Therefore disputed he in the synagogue with the devout persons and in the market daily with them that met with him. Then certain philosophers of the Epicureans, and of the Stoicks, encountered him. And some said, What will this babbler say? others said, He seemeth to be a setter forth of strange gods" (Acts 17:17, 18).

On the rock called the Areopagus, or Mars' Hill, opposite the Acropolis, Paul gave his famous speech to the Athenians: "Ye men of Athens, I perceive that in all things ye are too superstitious. For as I passed by, and beheld your devotions, I found an altar with this inscription, TO THE UNKNOWN GOD. Whom therefore ye ignorantly worship, him declare I unto you. God that made the world and all things therein, seeing that he is Lord of heaven and earth, dwelleth not in temples made with hands . . ." (Acts 17:22-24).

The marketplace where Paul spoke was the Agora, located below the Acropolis. It must have been buzzing with political discussions, buying, selling, bargaining, donkeys braying, pigs squealing, poultry cackling. It was customary for Athenian men, rather than women, to go to the marketplace every day to purchase household supplies. As Athenian citizens wandered from one wicker booth to another gathering supplies, shopkeepers hawked their wares: "Buy my oil!" "Buy sausage!" "Buy charcoal!" The men were usually dressed in long white togas, but here and there could be seen blue, orange, green or brown cloaks trimmed with purple. Throughout what seemed to be total confusion was actually a pattern of orderly commerce. Certain areas dealt in specific foodstuffs. Some shopkeepers even provided snacks by cooking lentils and peas to order. One of the busiest booths was the bread center. Here old women sold their large cylinder-shaped loaves all stacked in neat piles. Another sought-after commodity was myrtle. Athenians loved to wear garlands around their heads, always fresh, and these were usually made from myrtle leaves. Fishmongers used a large part of the market, for the fish trade was superb and they carried every delectable sea food the Mediterranean, Aegean and Ionian seas offered.

When these fresh foods arrived home, housewives or servants prepared all kinds of interesting dishes. A Grecian woman who was a good cook might make a variety of stuffings for chicken or capon, from our onion-and-spice to bulgur wheat or rice. If she was from Corinth, she presumably had a favorite recipe using cream in her mashed turnips. We have suggested pita pockets in this menu because Paul and his missionaries were great travelers, and pita, filled with a variety of vegetables, preserved fish and cheese, traveled well, and made a nourishing lunch eaten along the road or near a shaded riverbank. Isthmus Wreath Cake is a mere play upon words but refers to the Isthmian games Paul mentions in First Corinthians 9:24: "Know ye not that they which run in a race run all, but one receiveth the prize? So run, that ye may obtain."

The working man's regular diet consisted of broth and a barley meal porridge, fresh and salted fish. Two-course dinners were usually served. For the first course he enjoyed fish, vegetables, a soup occasionally and meat if he could afford it. Many vegetables were cooked or eaten raw: peas, onions, radishes, asparagus, and garlic. Meats ranged from a fair share of poultry such as geese, doves, and partridges to a limited supply of beef, mutton, pork, or goat meat. Fish would have been chosen from sole, tunny, mackerel, mullet, turbot, carp, halibut, young shark, or even a delicacy of eels wrapped in beet leaves and cooked on the coals. Shellfish were popular—oysters, mussels, and snails, although snails were considered the poor man's salad. Sometimes a wife would prepare an omelet made with milk, eggs, flour, brains, fresh cheese and honey cooked in rich broth and served wrapped in a fig leaf. A dessert of fruits, sweetmeats and confections flavored with honey ended the dinner.

Aristophanes gives an interesting account of a poor man's meal, ". . . a cake bristling with bran for economy's sake, onion, dish of sow thistles or mushrooms served with wine and olive oil, also some other variety of vegetables." To most Greeks bread, oil and wine were the basic requirements. A working man in Athens usually began his day with a few pieces of bread dipped in undiluted wine. Bread was made from wheat, barley, rye, millet or spelt (a kind of wheat), preferably from the first two. They baked only the wheat flour into loaves; the barley meal was kneaded and eaten "raw" or like a porridge. The wheat loaves bought in the Agora were shaped into slender rolls, a medium-sized loaf or into enormous loaves made from two to three bushels of flour. All bread was served with olive oil, no butter.

A dinner party in Athenian society began rather late at night. As soon as a guest arrived he removed his sandals, servants washed his feet, presented him with a garland for his head and ushered him into the dining room lined with couches and plump, fluffy pillows. When all the guests were comfortably reclining on their couches, servants brought in a small table for each one. The main course was attractively set with egg dishes, fish, cheese, hare or pigeon and various vegetables, sausage and black pudding. Sometimes mutton or pork were prepared if either of these animals had been sacrificed that day. There were no knives or forks, just pieces of bread used as spoons and when they finished using the "spoons" they tossed them on the floor to be swept out between courses by the servants. When the entrée was over servants quickly removed the tables and brought them back for dessert—figs, cakes, sweetmeats, and fine wines.

Xenophon describes the after-dinner part of a banquet attended by Socrates and other friends. "When the tables were removed and the guests had poured a libation and sung a hymn, there entered a man from Syracuse to give them an evening's entertainment. He had with him a fine flute girl, a dancing girl, and a very handsome boy who was expert at the zither and at dancing."

JERUSALEM ALMOND CHICKEN

2 tablespoons butter
4 tablespoons flour
1½ cups rich chicken broth
½ cup heavy cream
Salt, pepper and Tabasco
sauce to taste
2 tablespoons grated horseradish
Grated rind of ½ lemon
3 cups cooked diced chicken
¾ cup toasted almonds
Pita Bread

To make a velouté sauce, melt butter in a heavy saucepan. Add flour and cook a moment to remove flat taste. Add broth and stir constantly until thick and smooth. Add cream and continue cooking until sauce is of velvety consistency. Season with salt, pepper, Tabasco sauce, horseradish and lemon rind. Combine the sauce with the chicken and half the almonds. Serve on toasted Pita Bread. Garnish with remaining almonds.

Makes 6 to 8 servings.

PITA POCKETS

Split Pita Bread in half, then open cut edges, leaving space or a "pocket" for sandwich fillings, such as:

1. Feta cheese seasoned with salt, nutmeg and oil. Add chopped cucumber and onion to taste. Stuff into pockets and chill.

2. Thinly sliced meat and thin slices of firm melon.

3. Spread bread with olive oil then add any selection of fish salad.

4. Spread bread generously with butter and fill with chick-pea salad.

Any combination of sandwich fillings is suitable for use in this hearty and wholesome bread.

CREAMED TURNIPS

4 cups cooked, mashed turnips
6 tablespoons butter
⅔ cup hot cream
Salt and pepper to taste

Combine all ingredients; mix well. This may be done easily in a blender. Additional cream may be needed to produce the desired texture.

Makes 6 to 8 servings.

ISTHMUS WREATH CAKE

1 cup whole maraschino cherries
1 pound pitted dates
3 cups walnut halves
3 eggs
¾ cup sugar
¾ cup flour
1 teaspoon baking powder
½ teaspoon salt
2 teaspoons vanilla
Grated rind of 1 orange

Place fruits and nuts in a large bowl. Beat eggs, adding sugar gradually. Add flour, baking powder and salt, then vanilla and orange rind. Pour over fruit-nut mixture and mix thoroughly. Generously butter a 6-cup ring mold and pour in the batter. Bake at 325 degrees 1½ hours. If top of cake becomes too brown, cover loosely with foil during the last 30 minutes of baking.

Makes 6 to 8 servings.

CHAPTER EIGHTEEN

AGRIPPA

"And on the morrow, when Agrippa was come, and Bernice, with great pomp, and was entered into the place of hearing . . . Paul was brought forth" (Acts 25:23).

Menu

CAESAREA OYSTERS

CHICKEN BREASTS

WITH

TAHINI

WHOLE ARTICHOKES

PISTACHIO ALMOND MOUSSE

HONEY CAKE

AGRIPPA

Agrippa, the last king of Judea, was a grandson of Herod the Great. Born in 10 B.C., he was brought to Rome by his mother after Herod had executed his father. Through his mother's family connections he was raised in the imperial household. The political and financial fortunes of this wily opportunist—in that, a true Herod—rose and fell in rapid succession. He was rescued from debtor's prison by his friend, Caligula, who bestowed on him the title of king and gave him almost all of his grandfather's Palestinian kingdom to rule. In Palestine Agrippa was enormously popular and was idolized for removing direct Roman rule and restoring the Herodian kingdom. In Jerusalem he showed every outward appearance of Jewish piety, even persecuting the followers of Jesus as heretics in order to appease the orthodox elements of the city.

Agrippa often visited the seaport city of Caesarea, the former Roman capital of Palestine, and here he played a vastly different role. At Caesarea he lived as a pagan in the Greek manner, displaying statues of himself and his daughters and striking coins with his portrait. This magnificent city had been rebuilt by Herod the Great, who spent twelve years constructing ornate palaces and public buildings, all of white marble. His most impressive achievement was the building of a protected harbor which extended two hundred feet into the sea "that was always free of the waves of the sea," according to Josephus.

Caesarea was still the principal port of Palestine during Paul's day. From the surrounding seas came a variety of fresh seafood. King Agrippa of Caesarea enjoyed such luxuries as oysters and lobsters with truffles. It is reported that over one hundred different kinds of pastry were prepared at Caesarea. (These were not the sweet pastries we know today.

Many were made of light egg bread dough flavored with honey and spices and baked in different shapes.) Wealthy Romans had also discovered the secret of primitive refrigeration. According to Pliny "Some people . . . turn what is the curse of mountain regions into pleasure for their appetites. Coolness is stored up against the hot weather, and plans are devised to keep snow cold for the months that are strangers to it. Other people first boil their water and then bring even that to a winter temperature. Assuredly mankind wants nothing to be as nature likes to have it." Our recipe for Pistachio Almond Mousse illustrates this point.

Paul passed through Caesarea on his way to celebrate the ancient feast of Pentecost in Jerusalem. There his preaching against Judaic customs antagonized the priests, and a charge was brought against Paul that he had defiled the temple by allowing gentiles into the sacred inner confines. Because of his Roman citizenship he was placed under protective custody by the Romans, who transferred him back to Caesarea for safekeeping after a group of Jewish fanatics had sworn to assassinate him. The apostle insisted on his rights as a Roman citizen and demanded a hearing before the Emperor. Paul's last court appeal in Caesarea was tried before Agrippa. "Then said Agrippa unto Festus, This man might have been set at liberty, if he had not appealed unto Caesar" (Acts 26:32). Under the guard of a centurion Paul was placed on a ship bound for Rome.

Agrippa

CAESAREA OYSTERS
(Oyster Casserole)

1 large onion
4 stalks celery
1 green pepper
¼ pound butter
3 tablespoons flour
1 cup milk
Salt, white pepper and Tabasco sauce
1½ quarts shelled oysters, drained
6 slices toast
3 tablespoons parsley

Chop vegetables fine, discarding seeds and white membranes of the green pepper. Melt butter in a large skillet and sauté the vegetables until limp. Sprinkle flour over and mix thoroughly. Add milk and cook until mixture is thickened. Season to taste. When ready to serve, add oysters and cook a few minutes or until the edges curl (about 2 to 3 minutes). Do not overcook. Serve very hot on crisp toast. Garnish with parsley.

Makes 6 to 8 servings.

CHICKEN BREASTS WITH TAHINI

4 tablespoons butter or margarine
2 tablespoons diced onion
¾ cup diced celery
2 cups cooked rice
⅓ cup tahini (sesame seed paste)
Salt and pepper to taste
Grated rind of 1 orange
6 boned chicken breasts
½ cup flour
2 cups chicken broth
1 tablespoon cornstarch
1½ tablespoons cold water
1 cup seedless grapes, cut in half

Melt 2 tablespoons butter or margarine in a large skillet and sauté onion and celery lightly. Add rice and toss to coat with butter. Stir in tahini. Season to taste with salt, pepper and orange peel. Pound chicken breasts between pieces of wax paper. Fill each with about 1 tablespoon of the rice mixture and roll up. Dredge each roll in flour and brown in remaining 2 tablespoons butter. Place rolls in a shallow casserole and add broth. Simmer 20 minutes. Remove chicken to a heated serving platter. Mix cornstarch with water and add to pan juices. Cook until thickened. Add grapes to sauce. Correct seasonings and pour over chicken.

Makes 6 to 8 servings.

WHOLE ARTICHOKES

6 large artichokes
1 teaspoon salt
2 tablespoons olive or salad oil
1 tablespoon lemon juice
1 clove garlic

Remove stems and tough outer leaves from artichokes. Cut off about 1 inch from tops of each and discard. In large saucepan, place artichoke in 1 inch boiling water; add remaining ingredients. Simmer covered, 30 to 45 minutes or until tender when pierced at the stem end. If preferred, boil artichokes in salted water to cover for about 20 minutes. Drain and cool. Serve with Basic Salad Dressing or hollandaise sauce.

Makes 6 servings.

PISTACHIO ALMOND MOUSSE

1 teaspoon butter
¼ cup shredded almonds
2 cups heavy cream
⅓ cup honey
Few drops of almond extract
Dash of salt
¼ cup shelled chopped pistachio nuts

Melt butter in a small skillet. Add almonds and toss until golden. Set aside to cool. Whip cream until stiff, gradually adding honey, almond extract and salt. Fold in almonds and pistachio nuts. Place in an airtight container and freeze.

Makes 6 to 8 servings.

HONEY CAKE

1½ cups flour
1 cup sugar
Dash of salt
1 teaspoon ground ginger
1 teaspoon cinnamon
½ teaspoon ground mace
1 teaspoon soda
3 tablespoons oil
1 cup honey
3 eggs
Grated rind of 1 lemon
½ cup chopped candied orange peel
¼ cup slivered almonds

Combine dry ingredients in a large bowl. Heat oil and honey together until just warm. Add with remaining ingredients except almonds to the dry mixture. Stir well to combine. Pour batter into a buttered 9-inch pie plate. Bake at 350 degrees 40 minutes or until cake is springy to the touch. Sprinkle slivered almonds on top of the cake. Allow to cool before cutting.

Makes a 9-inch cake.

CHAPTER NINETEEN

NERO, EMPEROR OF ROME

Menu

PALATINE HORS D'OEUVRE

VEAL BIRDS

GNOCCHI WITH SALSA VERDE

BAKED EGGPLANT SLICES

PLUM MOUSSE

NERO, EMPEROR OF ROME

According to scholars, Paul arrived in Rome about A.D. 60 during the reign of Nero and lived "two whole years in his own hired house" (Acts 28:30). Although he was kept under surveillance, he was allowed to preach and write.

Romans who lived during this era were well traveled, well informed and well educated. Travel was made relatively easy and inexpensive by the extensive network of roads throughout the Empire, a masterpiece of Roman skill and organization. Plutarch, in his *On Exile,* describes the citizens of Rome as "globetrotters who spend the best part of their lives in inns and on boats."

A concomitant of this ease of travel was the expansion of the import trade. Wealthy Romans considered crops raised in Italy unfit for their consumption and ate only imports. Imagine a Roman epicure shop stocked with only the finest imports: cereals and grain from the Black Sea, Sicily and Egypt; wheat from Britain, Germany and Spain; ginger and cinnamon from Arabia; pepper and many other spices from India; citron from West Africa; figs from Asia Minor and Syria; apples, pears, plums, dates, pomegranates and nuts from Syria; cherries from the Black Sea and cheeses from Gaul.

Excessive eating became the gastronomic fashion of the times—if one could afford it. Fabulous sums were spent on individual banquets. Many a Roman ruined himself financially because of his elaborate table. If a fashionable dinner party were to be given, perhaps by the emperor Nero, it would begin with fancy *hors d'oeuvres*—mussels, field fares, thrushes and other song birds with asparagus, fattened fowls, oyster pastries, sea nettles, ribs of roe and purple shellfish. The dinner proper might include sows' udders, a boar's head, dishes of fish livers, flamingoes' tongues, or peacocks' brains and pheasants mixed together. It was not uncommon for the main course of such a banquet to include over twenty different dishes. Elaborate desserts finished the meal.

Entertainment was an integral part of such a banquet. The tables were beautifully decorated with flowers and sometimes sprigs of parsley. The air was sprayed with perfume. Often, hosts gave gifts to their guests. At some parties guests were surprised by perfumes and flowers falling from the ceiling. Music, dancing and a staged tableau might cap an extravagant party. When Nero entertained in Rome, he and his friends turned themselves into an amateur poetry society after dinner. Nero also enjoyed participating in acting and theatricals as the theatre was one of his great loves.

He must have been a tyrannical performer. Once in Greece, he gave a series of singing performances accompanied by the harp, and was always prepared to play the flute and bagpipes followed by a dance. Whenever he performed, the doors of the theatre were locked so that no one could leave. People often became so weary of listening and applauding they would go to great lengths to escape, sometimes jumping from the theater walls or playing dead in order to be carried out.

Our Nero menu modestly reflects a small portion of the enormous banquets prepared in his Golden House on the Palatine. Nero's vanity was famous, his self-indulgence extreme. That is why our menu is pure whimsy, with the emphasis on royal purple.

PALATINE HORS D'OEUVRE
(Composed Salad)

4 hard-cooked eggs
1 cup beet juice
1 package frozen artichoke hearts
2 to 3 cups shredded red cabbage
4 tablespoons black caviar
Palace Dressing (recipe follows)

Peel eggs, leaving them whole. Allow them to soak in beet juice to color them purple. Cook artichoke hearts according to directions on package. Make individual nests of cabbage. Place several artichoke hearts in each nest. Cut each egg in half and place cut side down in center of each nest. Cover with dressing and garnish with caviar. Serve with Palace Dressing.

Makes 6 to 8 servings.

PALACE DRESSING

3 tablespoons mayonnaise
3 tablespoons olive oil
2 tablespoons vinegar
2 scallions, finely minced
Salt and Tabasco sauce

Combine mayonnaise, oil, vinegar and scallions; mix thoroughly. Add seasonings to taste.

Makes about 1 cup dressing.

Nero

VEAL BIRDS

6 very thin slices of veal leg
6 tablespoons butter
1 small onion or shallot, minced
1 cup packaged stuffing
4 tablespoons crumbled Roquefort cheese
2 tablespoons flour
½ pound mushrooms, sliced
1 cup chicken broth
Salt and pepper

Pound veal very thin between two sheets of wax paper. Heat 4 tablespoons butter in a heavy skillet and sauté onion or shallot until limp. Add stuffing and toss to coat with butter, then add the cheese. Roll mixture in veal slices; secure with toothpicks. Dust rolls with flour on all sides and brown in same skillet. Remove to a shallow casserole. Deglaze skillet with chicken broth, then pour it around the veal birds. Season to taste. Cover and simmer very gently 40 minutes. Remove wooden picks. Sauté mushrooms in remaining 2 tablespoons butter and serve with veal birds.

Makes 6 servings.

GNOCCHI WITH SALSA VERDE

2 cups flour
1 pound ricotta cheese
2 egg yolks
1 teaspoon salt
2 tablespoons Parmesan cheese, grated
2 quarts chicken broth
Melted butter (optional)
Parsley (optional)
Salsa Verde (recipe follows)

Place flour in large bowl. Make a well in the center and add ricotta cheese, egg yolks, salt and Parmesan cheese. Mix thoroughly with a wooden spoon, then knead the mixture until it becomes firm enough to form into tubular-shaped rolls about ½-inch thick. Cut rolls into 1½-inch lengths and simmer in chicken broth. Gnocchi will rise to top as they are cooked. Remove with a slotted spoon; drain well. Serve in a shallow dish. Season with melted butter and chopped parsley, or serve with Salsa Verde.

Makes 6 to 8 servings.

SALSA VERDE

½ cup olive oil
2 tablespoons vinegar
1 teaspoon prepared mustard
1 tablespoon chopped parsley
1 tablespoon chopped watercress
1 tablespoon chopped spinach
2 tablespoons chopped chives
Salt and freshly ground pepper

Combine oil, vinegar and mustard; mix thoroughly. Add remaining ingredients and season to taste. Serve with Gnocchi, salads or vegetables.

Makes 1 cup dressing.

BAKED EGGPLANT SLICES

2 medium eggplants
¼ pound butter, softened
Salt and pepper to taste
½ cup grated Parmesan cheese

Cut unpeeled eggplant into ⅜-inch slices. Spread both sides with softened butter. Preheat oven to 500 degrees. Place slices in a jelly-roll pan and bake for 10 to 12 minutes, being careful not to burn. Turn slices over and sprinkle with salt, pepper and cheese. Return to oven and glaze quickly under the broiler. Serve at once.

Makes 6 to 8 servings.

PLUM MOUSSE

1 can or jar (16 ounces) purple plums
1 cup cream
⅓ cup honey
A few drops of almond flavoring
Dash of salt

Drain plums thoroughly. Use juice for other purposes. Chop fruit, removing seeds. Whip cream, adding honey gradually. Add almond flavoring and salt. Fold in chopped plums. Chill well and serve in sherbet glasses; or freeze, cut into slices and serve on dessert plates.

Makes 6 to 8 servings.

CHAPTER TWENTY

AGAPE

"There are spots in your feasts of charity [agape], when they feast with you, feeding themselves without fear: clouds they are without water, carried about of winds; trees whose fruit withereth . . . to whom is reserved the blackness of darkness forever" (Jude 1:12, 13).

Menu

EGGPLANT CASSEROLE

ICHTHYS

(BAKED STUFFED SNAPPER)

WHOLE-GRAIN BREAD

CHILLED CUSTARD

AGAPE

In New Testament Greek, the word *agape* is used to express the meaning of divine love. It is also the name for a love feast celebrated by early Christians, a feast observed with prayers, songs and scriptural readings. The tradition of such a feast may have originated in the meals Jesus had with his disciples or perhaps specifically from his feeding the multitude by the Sea of Galilee (Mark 6:34-44). The members of the early church provided meals for the poor and the widowed of the Christian community. These gatherings developed into ritualistic meetings, love feasts as shown in paintings on the walls of the catacombs of Domitilla and Priscilla in Rome.

The religious aspects of agape feasts gradually diminished and were replaced by decadent revelry. Such practices elicited strong censure from early church leaders such as Paul, who admonished the people about their participation (Jude 1:12, 13—used at beginning of chapter).

It is not until the end of the second century that scholars find detailed descriptions of the agape feasts.

Tertullian, a convert to Christianity, included rules of behavior in the *Apology* (A.D. 445-520) "Before reclining at table the banqueters first taste the food of prayer to God. Only so much is eaten as will satisfy hunger; only so much is drunk as will meet the needs of the modest. Their conversation is that of those who know the Lord is listening. After the water is brought for the ablutions of the hands (after dinner), the lights are brought in and each is asked to stand forth before the others and sing the praise of God, either from his own heart or from the Holy Scriptures. This also is evidence of how little we drink. Then the banquet ends, as it began, with prayer."

Food at the agape meals was simple—fish, bread, vegetables and fruit. Before sundown a family or group of friends gathered in a home to begin the observance with *hors d'oeuvres.* Then the group would surround a table, reclining or sitting, and the leader would give a benediction or thanksgiving to God, while the bread was broken.

The beautiful prayer that traditionally ended the Agape Feast is found in an early Christian prayer book. "Thou Almighty Master, didst create all things for Thy Name's sake and didst give food and drink to men for enjoyment, that they might render thanks to Thee; but didst bestow upon us spiritual food and drink and eternal life through Thy Servant. Above all, we give thanks to Thee that thou art mighty. To Thee be glory forever! Let grace come and let this world pass away! Amen."

EGGPLANT CASSEROLE

(Ratatouille)

½ cup olive oil
1 cup thinly sliced onions
2 cloves garlic, minced
½ cup pitted black olives, coarsely chopped
3 cups eggplant, peeled and sliced
3 cups zucchini, cubed
Salt and pepper

In a heavy skillet, heat oil and lightly sauté onion and garlic. Add olives, eggplant and zucchini. Toss to coat with oil, then allow to simmer until vegetables are just tender (approximately 20 minutes). Do not overcook. Season to taste. Serve hot or cold.

Note: Tomatoes are a fine addition to this dish, but were not in cultivation during these times. If you wish, add 4 large tomatoes, peeled and chopped, with the eggplant.

Makes 6 to 8 servings.

ICHTHYS

(Baked Stuffed Snapper)

½ cup olive oil
1 onion, minced
1 clove garlic, minced (optional)
½ cup chopped celery
⅓ cup chopped seeded cucumber
1 cup fine bread crumbs
Salt, pepper and nutmeg
Juice of 2 lemons
Grated rind of 1 lemon
1 red snapper (4 pounds)
Lemon slices

Heat oil in a large skillet. Add onion and garlic, cooking gently until onion is transparent. Stir in celery, cucumber and crumbs, tossing to coat thoroughly. Season to taste. Add juice and grated rind of one lemon. Stuff cavity of the fish with this mixture. Bake fish in a shallow pan at 350 degrees for about 40 minutes. Sprinkle remaining lemon juice over top of fish during baking. Garnish with thin slices of lemon.

Makes 6 to 8 servings.

WHOLE-GRAIN BREAD

2 packages active dry yeast
½ cup lukewarm water
1 cup uncooked quick-cooking oatmeal
2 teaspoons salt
2 tablespoons oil
3 cups boiling water
½ cup honey
1 cup bran
1 cup whole-wheat flour
6 to 7 cups unbleached flour
1 cup raisins (optional)
Melted butter

Dissolve yeast in lukewarm water. Combine oatmeal, salt, oil and boiling water. Allow to cool to lukewarm, then add yeast and honey. Stir in the bran, whole-wheat flour and enough unbleached flour to make a soft dough. Raisins may be added at this point. Turn dough out on a floured board, cover with a damp towel and allow to rest 5 minutes. Knead 8 to 10 minutes or until dough is smooth and elastic. If needed, add small amounts of unbleached flour to prevent stickiness. Place dough in a greased bowl, cover with a damp towel and allow to rise in a draft-free place until doubled in bulk, about 1½ hours. Punch down, divide in half and allow to rest again for 10 minutes. Form into 2 loaves and place in 2 well-greased 9×5×3-inch loaf pans, or form into 2 round loaves and bake on a greased baking sheet. Brush tops of dough with melted butter, cover and allow to rise until well rounded and puffy (about 50 minutes). Bake at 350 degrees for 55 to 60 minutes. Tap the bottom of loaves to test for doneness (they should sound hollow). Remove from pans at once and cool on wire racks.

Makes 2 loaves.

CHILLED CUSTARD

1 tablespoon flour
½ teaspoon salt
⅔ cup sugar
2 cups milk
3 eggs, separated
1 teaspoon vanilla

Combine flour, salt and sugar in a heavy saucepan. Gradually add milk and slightly beaten egg yolks. Cook over medium heat, stirring constantly with a wire whisk. When custard begins to thicken, reduce heat and cook only until mixture coats a spoon well, about 10 minutes. Do not overcook. Allow to cool. Beat egg whites until stiff, flavor with vanilla and fold into custard. Chill before serving.

Note: If custard is to be used as a dessert sauce, omit beaten whites.

Makes 6 to 8 servings.

ILLUSTRATIONS

BIBLIOGRAPHY

The Holy Bible. King James Version.

Buttrick, George A. *The Interpreter's Bible*. Vols. 7, 9. New York: Abingdon Press. 1962.

_________ ed. *The Interpreter's Dictionary of the Bible*. New York: Abingdon Press. 1962.

Hastings Dictionary of the Bible. New York: Charles Scribner's Sons. 1963.

Smith, William. *Smith's Bible Dictionary*. New York: Pyramid Books. 1967.

Abbott, John, S. C. and Russel, B. B. *The History of Christianity*. American Publishing Company. 1872.

Albright, William Foxwell. *From the Stone Age to Christianity*. New York: Doubleday, Anchor Books. 1957.

Allen, D. C. *The Legend of Noah*. Illinois: University of Illinois Press. 1963.

Apicius. *Cook Book, A.D. 24*. Old Tappan, New Jersey: Fleming H. Revell. 1958.

Charlesworth, Martin Percival. *Trade Routes and Commerce of the Roman Empire*. Cambridge, England: Cambridge University Press. 1924.

Crispo, Dorothy. *The Story of Our Fruits and Vegetables*. New York: Dorex House. 1968.

Dickson, H. R. P. *The Arab of the Desert*. London: Allen and Unwin, Ltd. 1951.

Durant, Will. *The Story of Civilization. Caesar and Christ*. Vol. 3. New York: Simon & Schuster, Inc. 1944.

_________. *The Story of Civilization. Our Oriental Heritage*. Vol. 1. New York: Simon & Schuster, Inc. 1954.

Encyclopedia Judaica. 2nd printing. Jerusalem. Vols. 5, 6, 7, 8, 11, 13. 1973.

Farrar, Frederic W. *Lives of the Fathers.* Vols. 1, 2. New York: Macmillan, Inc. 1889.

Flower, Barbara and Rosenbaum, Elizabeth. *Apicius.* London: G. G. Hannap & Co., Ltd. 1958.

Gibbon, Edward. *The Decline and Fall of the Roman Empire.* Vols. II, III. New York: Heritage Press. 1946.

Goor, Asaph and Nurock, Max. *The Fruits of the Holy Land.* Jerusalem; London; New York: Israel Universities Press. 1968.

Hawkes, Jaquetta, *The First Great Civilizations.* New York: Alfred A. Knopf, Inc. 1973.

Helbaek, Hans. *Plant Economy in Ancient Lachish.* Vol. IV.

Johnston, Mary. *Roman Life.* Illinois: Scott, Foresman and Co. 1957.

Josephus, Flavius. *Jewish Antiquities,* Vols. XIV, XV.

Kaloyeropoulou, Athena G. *Ancient Corinth.* Athens: M. Pechlivanidis & Co., Ltd.

Keller, Werner. *The Bible as History.* New York: William Morrow & Co., Inc. 1956.

________. *The Bible as History in Pictures.* New York: William Morrow & Co., Inc. 1963.

Kenyon, Kathleen. *Archaeology in the Holy Land.* New York: Praeger Publishing. 1970.

King, Eleanor. *Bible Plants for American Gardens.* New York: Macmillan, Inc. 1941.

Leonard, Jonathan Norton. *The Emergence of Man: The First Farmers.* Boston: Little, Brown and Co. 1973.

Macalister, R. A. S. *The Excavation of Gezer.* Vol. II. Boston. 1912.

Mazar, B. *The Excavation in the Old City of Jerusalem Near the Temple Mount.* Preliminary Report of the Second and Third Seasons, 1969-1970. Jerusalem: The Institute of Archaeology, Hebrew University. 1971.

Meinardus, Otto F. A. *St. Paul in Greece.* Athens: Lycabettus Press. 1972.

Neeman, D., and Sapir, B. (authors and publishers). *Capernaum.* Tel-Aviv: The Historical Sites Library. 1967.

Negev, Dr. Avraham. *Caesarea.* Tel-Aviv: E. Lewin-Epstein Ltd. 1967.

Parmelee, Alice. *All the Birds of the Bible, Their Stories, Identification and Meaning.* New York: Harper & Row. 1959.

Paul, Shalom M., and Dever, William G. *Biblical Archaeology.* Jerusalem: Keter Publishing House, Ltd. 1973.

The Reader's Digest Association. *Great People of the Bible and How They Lived.* Pleasantville, New York. 1974.

Stager, Lawrence E., Walker, Pinta and Wright, G. Ernest. *American Expedition to Idalion and Cyprus.* Cambridge, England: American School of Oriental Research. 1974.

Tannahill, Reay. *Food in History.* New York: Stein and Day. 1973.

Tertullian. *Apology.* From the Ante-Nicene Fathers, Part 1. Translations of the Writings of the Fathers down to A.D. 325. Vol. III. New York: Charles Scribner's Sons.

Trever, John C. *The Untold Story of Qumram.* Old Tappan, New Jersey: Fleming H. Revell Company. 1965.

Tucker, T. G. *Life in the Roman World of Nero and St. Paul.* New York: Macmillan, Inc. 1924.

Walker, Winifred. *All the Plants of the Bible.* New York: Harper & Row. 1957.

Wilkinson, Sir. J. Gardner. *Popular Account of the Ancient Egyptians.* Vols. I, II. New York: Harper and Row. 1854.

Yadin, Yigael. *Masada.* New York: Random House. 1966.

INDEX

Index

Approximate Conversions from Metric Measures

Symbol	When You Know	Multiply by	To Find	Symbol
		MASS (weight)		
g	grams	0.035	ounces	oz
kg	kilograms	2.2	pounds	lb
		VOLUME		
ml	milliliter	0.03	fluid ounces	fl oz
l	liters	2.1	pints	pt
l	liters	1.06	quarts	qt
l	liters	0.26	gallons	gal
		TEMPERATURE (exact)		
°C	Celsius temperature	9/5 then add 32	Fahrenheit temperature	°F